How to R..... Credit Score

Proven Strategies to Repair Your Credit Score, Increase Your Credit Score, Overcome Credit Card Debt and Increase Your Credit Limit

Complete Volume

By

Income Mastery

How to Raise Your Credit Score

Proven Strategies to Repair Your Credit Score, Increase Your Credit Score, Overcome Credit Card Debt and Increase Your Credit Limit

Volume 1

How to Raise Your Credit Score

Proven Strategies to Repair Your Credit Score, Increase Your Credit Score, Overcome Credit Card Debt and Increase Your Credit Limit

Volume 2

How to Raise Your Credit Score

Proven Strategies to Repair Your Credit Score, Increase Your Credit Score, Overcome Credit Card Debt and Increase Your Credit Limit

Volume 3

for any difficulties or damages that may occur to them after making the information presented here.

In addition, the information on the following pages is intended for informational purposes only and should therefore be regarded as universal. As befits its nature, it is presented without warranty with respect to its prolonged validity or provisional quality. The trademarks mentioned are made without written consent and can in no way be considered as sponsorship of the same.

Table of Contents

How to Raise your Credit Score: Volume 1

Proven Strategies to Repair Your Credit Score, Increase Your Credit Score, Overcome Credit Card Debt and Increase Your Credit Limit

By

Income Mastery

Introduction

The following book is written with the goal of providing information as accurate and reliable as possible. In any case, the purchase of this book takes into account that both the publisher and the author are not experts in the topics covered and that the recommendations or suggestions made here are for entertainment purposes only. Professionals should be consulted as necessary before undertaking any of the actions mentioned here.

This statement is considered fair and valid by both the American Bar Association and the Committee of the Publishers Association and is considered legal throughout the United States.

In addition, the transmission, duplication or reproduction of any of the following works, including specific information, shall be considered an illegal act regardless of whether it is in electronic or printed form. This extends to the creation of a secondary or tertiary copy of the work or a recorded copy and is only permitted with the express written consent of the author. All additional rights reserved.

The information on the following pages is generally considered to be a truthful and accurate description of the facts and, as such, any lack of attention, use or misuse of the information in question by the reader will cause the resulting actions to be solely within his or her competence. There are no scenarios in which the publisher or author of this book can be held liable for any difficulties or damages that may occur after the information presented here has been realized.

In addition, the information on the following pages is intended for informational purposes only and should therefore be regarded as universal. As befits its nature, it is presented without warranty with respect to its prolonged validity or provisional quality. The trademarks mentioned are made without written consent and can in no way be considered as sponsorship of the same.

Chapter 1: Credit History

Few of us know all the details involved in going to a bank and applying for a credit card, because that so-called credit history will be one of your best presentation letters or on the contrary will represent the great obstacle between your projects and your finances. What is credit history? It is the research that all financial institutions do before granting a loan. This prior investigation is based on the payment history and behavior of the applicant as well as the natural or legal person requesting it.

Likewise, we must know the term delinquency which implies the set of overdue credits, and they are considered overdue credits when the date of payment of the installments arrives, these are not canceled or when they only amortize a part of the amount established as installment.

In other words, your credit history will reflect both the positive credit that is the payments made on time, as well as delinquency, all according to the way you manage your finances and the driving you give your credits. For the granting or consent of credits, a method has been developed called in many economic studies such as the 5 C's, which are no more than five simple and basic conditions that serve for the analysis of the level of granting that the applicant may or may not have, and depending on these conditions, he/she will be able to opt for the granting of a credit for the first time or a new credit.

These 5 C´s correspond to the initials of five concepts used in the field of finance and the economy. It is qualitative to analyze each client individually to determine credit risk based on five factors which are of a character or commitment, capacity, capital, collateral, and conditions. Below we will explain in the simplest possible way:

CHARACTERISTICS

This character or commitment has to do directly with the fulfillment of the credit obligations that have been acquired throughout our life in different spheres, for example in commercial premises for the purchase of any electrical appliance or furniture. The best way to measure character is based on the applicant's payment history, i.e. it will be proportional to the timely fulfillment and the expected time of the item you have purchased.

As far as character is concerned, we analyze the honesty, morality, and integrity of the client in the fulfillment of their commitments and obligations and with third parties, how suitable you are at the time of canceling your goods as a client. This is the most important aspect of the model because it allows us to determine the degree of responsibility and credibility of the client in terms of their payments.

CAPACITY.

We define capacity as the amount of service that can be obtained in a certain productive unit during a certain period of time. We consider capacity as a medium or long-term decision, that is, at least it will not change in the next two years. In a few words, determine the diversity of assistance or uses of services that you require for the maintenance of your personnel or if it is referred to your company.

When analyzing capacity, the aim is to determine whether the client has sources of income that allow it to cover all of its costs and expenses, including its financial and economic commitments to banks and suppliers or creditors. This factor is generally measured using historical cash flow analysis and projected cash flow estimates. This is a determining factor in deciding whether or not to approve credit, since credit can only be granted to clients who demonstrate that they can pay for it, i.e., that they are financially solvent.

CAPITAL

Capital is the number of resources, goods, and values available to satisfy a need or carry out a defined activity and that generate an economic benefit or profit for you or your partners and shareholders in the case of having a company in economics, capital is defined as an element of the production you have. We can also say that capital is the nominal value of the shares issued by a company and subscribed by the partners. According to the percentage of participation in the company, you can define the specific political and economic weight of your capital as well as that of the company.

In this sense, the capital factor of the client, seeks to determine the financial position, the relationship between their assets and liabilities contracted, to know the ability they have to contract new debts and bear losses, this does not only apply when you own a business but in your finances.

COLLATERAL

Expressed as collateral refers to your assets and possessions that you must have as an applicant for credit, and this collateral must be valued at the same cost you are requesting on the credit. The guarantee that can be sold or seized in the event of non-payment is that the financial institution has the power to sell your property or simply keep it to cover the amount of debt acquired through the credit granted. The value of the collateral depends on the disposal cost and possible resale value.

In this sense, collateral refers to evaluating the assets that will be taken as collateral for the credit. Banks take the client's assets, mainly to constitute preferred or real guarantees, as support for the commitment and fulfillment of the credit payment.

TERMS AND CONDITIONS

The general economic conditions of your possessions and personal assets such as those of your company will directly affect or support the decision to grant credit. On the other hand, also economic conditions external to you or your business as an improvement or deterioration of general economic conditions in terms of the country's financial stability, inflation levels can cause interest rates to change or the risk of granting credit. Also, the conditions of a particular industry can affect the profitability of granting credit to a company in this type of industry, this will depend on the type of venture you have, does not necessarily apply in all.

In terms of conditions, the aim is to determine the external aspects that influence the use and return of credit. The situation of the economy, the political and social environment, the sector in which the client operates, the level of competition, etc. This method is highly subjective, as it does not analyze the strategic position or the ratios provided by the client's financial accounting information. Just as the previous method cannot be applied to entrepreneurs or microentrepreneurs, financial information is not available and if their assets are not healthy in the vast majority of cases.

Now, from the development of your 5 C's, will be formulated the judgment about your credit quality, it is for all the above mentioned that it is important to know and have a positive credit history along with the proper management of these resources with an appropriate and viable planning, especially as you owe to your workforce which will always be a motivation to fulfill your role with greater responsibility, and thus optimizing those financial resources in a sustainable way and that yields the best results. Therefore, the good management of your resources, the fulfillment of the acquired credit responsibilities added to an adequate analysis of the credit risk can reconcile in your favor to obtain the resources that you need to have before a financial entity to achieve optimal results with your credit card.

On the other hand, it is not too much to know the analysis position of the financial or banking agency for granting credits, this analysis position refers to the credit process called 5 P´s. The credit process 5 P´s is a subtle approach to resolving facts, giving responsible opinions and circumventing few clear factors in a risk assessment process: credit, to arrive at a granting decision.

Therefore 5P´s is a process that is characterized by a sequence of steps or by being composed of several elements, in this case, are personal, purpose, payment, protection and perspective. It is important to have a clear understanding of this to get the most out of it. Here are some of the key features of 5P´s:

PERSONAL

This is considered under two simple perspectives: the first is whether applicants are responsible and successful and whether they treat their bankers and creditors fairly and equally. The information about the borrower, in this case, you, must have three characteristics: Complete (human element), Truthful (Comment research), Updated (accounting information). In short, the personnel to be considered are from two approaches: those of the personnel conducting the analysis and research on the applicant and that of the applicant itself, which is why all information from the parties involved must be true, complete, legal and up to date.

PURPOSE

It is necessary to have proof of the destination of the credit, that is to say where the money is directed or destined. It is basic to being able to establish your payment plan, i.e., how it will be repaid, the repayment term and the interest rate.

Serves for the lender to observe the degree of risk as they can be high or low. The purposes of the credit can be directed to natural persons as well as to companies and industries in general.

PAYMENT

The payment is a derivation of the purpose and as such must be appropriate for the borrower and also for the creditor within the normal term of the loan. The source and time of repayment should be analyzed and it should be convinced that the probability of repayment is high. You should know your Cash Flow and when your business will contract or expand depending on your future vision and likelihood.

Payment is considered to be one of the most important and essential parts when making the credit of any kind since there must be an agreement between all parties, i.e. the financial institution and the credit applicant. There are terms of payment that determine the precise amounts and time of payment. It is also of fundamental relevance to investigate the applicant's capacity, that is to say, the capacity that you acquire for your income when canceling your debts.

PROTECTION

A properly structured loan includes an alternative, having protection or the second exit in case the primary payment source fails. Protection can be:

Internal: where the lender looks exclusively at the taker.

External: when a third party assumes credit responsibility to the policyholder.

Collateral is analyzed from the point of view of liquidity, which is nothing more than the ease with which a good can be transformed into money.

PERSPECTIVE

It is understood in the sense that credit can have from the basic analysis to assume the risk and earn the reward that frames the *business*. The main alternatives to the prospect of not accepting risk are: Avoid and/or hedge risks, there are appropriate instruments such as swaps, forward transactions (Forward), in addition to portfolio diversification. Reduce risk or prevent losses and adapt various actions or preventions.

Some of the most important factors most often taken into account in calculating your credit rating are usually the following:

- Payment History: is an accurate description of all payments without exception, including late payments, accounts on which there is a record of late payments, and negative legal actions, such as bankruptcy. All this makes up 35% of your rating and is all the movements you have made with the flow of your money.

- Accounts Payable: This includes the types of accounts, the balances, the total debt, the ratio of debt to available credit, and the percentage of debt remaining in installments, i.e., all of the payment responsibility you have at the time. This makes up 30% of your score.

- Credit history age: This takes into account the age of your credit accounts (from the oldest to the most recent transaction you've made), the average age of all your credit accounts, and the frequency of use of each of them. This makes up 15% of your score.

- Types of Credit: This includes the financial or banking institutions from which you received credit and the dates you received it, as well as all pertinent information from them and makes up 10% of your score.

- New Credits: Applying for multiple credits negatively affects your credit score unless all applications have been made recently, i.e., within 30 days. This makes up 10% of your score.

Chapter 2: What Do We Know as Credit Risk?

Credit risk is the probability that the counterparty, i.e. you as the debtor, may have the character of a natural or legal person, by not fulfilling your obligations under the agreed terms; i.e., the risk that a debtor will not pay the financial institution (IFI) the monthly payments or the loan granted on the agreed date.

We can state that the credit risk is not limited to the loan function acquired through credit cards, but includes other functions performed by a financial institution, including the extension of commitments and guarantees, bank acceptances, interbank loans, foreign exchange transactions, among other options, therefore the failure to make payments to your credit card will directly affect all operations or requirements. In short, failure to make payments on your financial commitments, whether to your credit card, commercial creditors and cooperative creditors, or any other form of a legal loan, will have an impact on your creditworthiness.

Therefore, the lack of creditworthiness will not only affect the possibility of obtaining any other banking service, but also any banking transaction will be affected. If you do not have the required payment capacity, it will be deducted from your banking transactions, be it payroll payments or third party deposits, and finally, it will even have repercussions on your ability to keep your goods and possessions.

It is for this reason that the best way to avoid a loss of your capital or your assets is to know the risks you run at the moment of managing any type of loan up to the use of your credit card, since through this you can visualize the possibilities of future payment that you must comply with, this is known as credit risk. A good credit risk analysis includes planning, organization, direction, and control.

Your ability to pay as a client is judged by an analysis of expected revenue streams during the loan period and the debtor's ability to meet its future financial needs. These factors can be affected by both the economic environment and the customer's environment.

In this sense, we can say that the credit evaluation has a high degree of a negative relationship with the level of credit risk because the better the credit is evaluated, the lower the probability that the client will delay or stop paying his credit.

Tips you can follow that can help lower your credit risk:

- Always check your credit information after requesting free reports, you can usually order additional credit reports easily from any of the major credit reporting agencies for a more convenient fee or in some cases even access your credit information for free at the online address of the financial institution of which you are apart. Having in order and knowing all your information will give you a better opinion regarding your finances.

- Each of the accounts on your credit report is classified by a letter and number that also indicates the type of account you have. For example, in the USA, an account classified as I1 means that it is an individual account that is paid on time. If your account is classified as J1, this means it is a *joint* account. An account classified as I5 can be a problem for you. Therefore, prioritize all accounts classified with numbers greater than 1 and everything that has been allocated to collection agencies, this will always depend on where you are since not all agencies have the same parameters at the time of classification.

- If you're thinking of purchasing either a house or a car and want to get much lower rates, search within 30 days so that your credit applications don't negatively affect your credit score and you can benefit from it.

- You should keep in mind that if a lender refuses to give you credit or changes the terms of the original agreement that have already been agreed upon, they are required to provide you with your credit rating.

- If at any time you dispute something in your credit report, the agency must notify you in writing of what is found in its investigation and send you a free copy of the report if this results in a change in the report.

- If you acquire additional money the best option will be to use it to pay off first all the debts you have with the priority of those who have the highest interest rates. This is called the avalanche method, in which you cancel the payments needed to keep your accounts current and pay your overdue bills, starting with the one that has the highest interest with any excess in your cash flow. In the long run, this will save you money and is the fastest way to pay off all of your debts and they don't keep increasing over time.

Chapter 3: How to Recover Your Credit History Infallible Strategies for Financially Recovering Yourself

At this point you will have understood the importance of having a good credit history for everything you want to do, but that perfect state of things do not last forever, sometimes fortuitous situations arise that force us to deal with emergencies of many kinds, medical, weather, accidents that will have a direct financial impact, forcing us to acquire debts beyond our payment possibilities or others such as the loss of our jobs or income, in short, situations that no one would like to have but we are not except that they occur or we get rid of them, there is no financial bubble that allows us never suffer for any of these inconveniences.

These unforeseen situations in many cases will alter our relationship with banking institutions affecting our credit history by putting us in a difficult situation with their collection offices, these situations cause payments to be delayed or not made in full. When this happens, people often file for bankruptcy in order to start from scratch, but this has a negative impact on their credit history for at least the next 7 years, and in the long run will bring further disadvantages.

Therefore, knowing how to fix or repair your credit situation is the best alternative to provide the emotional peace of mind you need and the financial credibility you need to pursue your dreams, plans and projects, ultimately with your future or plans in the short or medium term. That's why here are some proven strategies that can help you repair your credit plan:

1. Commitment: Fixing your credit condition involves making the necessary sacrifices, that involve differentiating between the basic needs that you cannot do without and the desires that you must suppress or ultimately discard. Your commitment lies in distinguishing what you can do without and what is not necessary. We know it's not easy, even the shortest way home is full of temptations but keep in mind that the greatest satisfaction will be when you can reward yourself with small details after you have settled all your debts and made a commitment to them.

2. Communicate: Involve the people you trust most, your family, friends, and even co-workers who help you, as well as everyone else who may be affected by your credit slide. You will need all the support of your social, family and patrimonial environment to direct the arrangement of your credit and improve it. Even more so if one of your relatives has contributed to the financial problem, either by going to their aid or for whatever cause. Be sincere and expose your situation and you will get the collaboration you need to make the solution more satisfactory in the end.

3. Plan: It is not easy to elaborate a budget when you do not have experience and above all to stick to this one, but to elaborate it and to take it as a rhythm of life will help you in all your plans. Take into account that a budget is nothing more than a detailed projection of what your income has been in order to allocate what part of it will go to your expenses, in what proportion you can implement a savings system and how to solve reasonably the debts that allow you to recover your credit credibility to obtain greater benefits from it.

For this you must know the amount of your fixed monthly expenses, i.e. the payment of housing, utilities and any other that you can not exclude for your survival and reasonably should not exceed 50% of your income so as to have 20% for your financial expenses which include the payment of loans, funds, and amortizations that you need to cancel. Finally, 30% of the monthly income must be directed to the payment of flexible expenses which consist of covering the required food, fuel and other necessary purchases such as medicines, of course, we should also talk about recreation and entertainment, but this will be a favorable area in time of economic solvency.

4. Consolidation: you must make immediate decisions such as moving away from the most expensive debts while still assuming their payment, for example in the case of credit cards, insurance payment, and short-term debts, the best way to overcome them is to cancel what is owed which will immediately strengthen your credit

profile. Ultimately you can go to a loan or mortgage to settle short-term debts allowing you to take care of their payment after consciously planning a real budget and be possible to pay later, but remember that any external help you seek to resolve it can be negative, make the best decisions to do so, do not fall into the vicious circle of indebtedness more to pay off old debts that ultimately only become new debts.

5. Check: keep up to date on the review of information issued by banks or your monthly statements of your credit accounts that will allow you to track real expenses made as well as is very important to realize any incorrect information of a transaction or omission of any payment, which can be negative in your favor. Only the periodic review of your reports will allow you to make the claims that are in place, taking into account that many of these reports have a period of no more than 30 days for any claim, therefore, you should contact the issuing entity immediately so that the relevant investigation is made and rectify their error and do not cause you more debts or these influence your net income.

6. Request: You need to keep your credit information up to date so you should request credit reports from credit bureaus, credit reporting agencies, banks, finance companies as well as installment buying centers or cooperatives, they are usually required to give you a free copy of your credit report once a year if you request it. Credit reports contain your credit score and your credit history, so businesses and lenders rely on them to

determine whether or not to give you credit and how much they will charge you in final interest.

7. Program: You'll find it helpful to schedule automatic debits to your bank account for your house and car payments, utilities and credit cards, which will help you make them on time in case you forget to do so. If this is not possible, you can schedule reminders for your payments on your cell phone calendar or in any software you use to monitor all of your expenses in a given period. Before scheduling automatic debits, be sure to coordinate them with the dates you receive deposits to your account to find a positive balance at the time of collections.

8. Change: In short, a real change of habits and attitude towards your financial reality will allow you to generate favorable credit balances, if on the contrary, you continue to make more expenses than your income supports, you will worsen the situation of risk of losing your credit credibility or even worse of declaring bankruptcy. Don't despair if you are faced with a completely unfavorable financial reality, remember that there are always ups and downs but that these may be recoverable.

9. Rectify: All debts can be negotiated, but the payment obligations agreed upon in principle are not negotiable, they will change until the creditor agrees in writing to the new terms. Before agreeing to a change in the terms of the loan, make sure you know how far you can go into

debt. Unfortunately, if you have a negative history, such as delinquencies or bankruptcies, they will affect your credit rating for years to come. However, you must be aware and clear of your real payment capacity before assuming any commitment, which will save you many inconveniences. Don't commit to more than you really can.

10. Constancy: taking care of overdue debts, although paying them will not help improve your credit rating since the important thing at that time is to pay the debt and get out of it as soon as possible. Therefore, paying off your oldest debts helps prevent collections from appearing on your credit report. On the other hand, assuming the acquired debts responsibly allows you to generate the proof required to demonstrate a positive credit history. To do this, you must prioritize your payments according to their seniority, their condition and the institution to which you must respond. Don't forget that all these situations will be reflected in your credit history and your net finances when wanting to do any future project.

11. Guarantee: Keep in mind that some institutions charge high interest if a portion of your credit card balance goes unpaid (even though you pay the entire balance when you make your initial deposit, thanks to the interest on the card) and also charge additional fees. So make sure you pay the full balance every month. Always guarantee your credit by obtaining guaranteed cards. These cards are a good option if you want to have a

credit card without having to worry about overspending. With this method, you deposit an amount of money to a lender and they issue you a card with that credit limit, this will be useful for you not to have more debts than you can not be responsible for the high amount to cancel.

Most banks and credit unions offer these types of loans, through which they borrow money, invest it in a savings account as collateral at the lending institution, and pay it off monthly through small payments. This helps to establish a credit history, in addition, the interest charged to the savings account is usually 2 to 3% less than those charged for the loan and you compensate the difference through your other sources of income, but keep in mind that you should not use this savings account for anything more than paying this loan. If you can, make additional payments using your income. This way, you'll reduce your outstanding balance and increase your savings to pay off all your debts.

12. Prudence: As your credit profile improves, new opportunities and new credit offers will inevitably arise. Don't trust the good streak you may have at that time, be prudent and watch out for high credits. Although having high credit indeed increases your credit rating and you have the possibility of assuming other types of risks if you are an entrepreneur, but using them often decreases it. Ideally, you should use a maximum of 30 to 15 % of your credit availability. For example, if your total credit card line is $20,000, do not incur a balance of more than $5,000 over an extended period of time.

13. Negotiate: Showing your face and being clear when talking about your circumstances does not make you less debtor but a better person and maybe you can make a difference when managing new payment agreements and even credit means. You should know who to pay each of your debts to and keep in touch with them. Be honest with your creditors. For example, you should notify them if you know you will have trouble paying a debtor that one of your payments will be late. Most likely they'll be willing to compromise. Accounts that are already overdue are listed on your credit report and will be reflected in your credit score, so it's best to keep your credit accounts up to date because this shows that you have good older credit sources rather than newer ones. When paying off overdue debts, explain to the creditor that you want to update your credit accounts and ask for help if necessary. Here are some things the creditor will be able to do for you:

- Allow you to pay your past due to balance over several months if you make future payments on time.

- Restore your account so that payments appear as current rather than past due. For this, an agreement must be drawn up and you must make sure you comply with the new payment terms.

- I may be able to waive any fees or penalties charged to your account.

14. Understand: You should take the time to identify the information provided by credit reports to verify that the commitments made are correct as well as the accuracy of the information they provide. Generally, free annual reports do not show your score but only the information used to calculate it.

This is the information that usually appears on your credit report:

- Identifying information: your name, address, social security number or equivalent where you live, date of birth, and employment information. This is not used to calculate your rating, but you must still make sure that this data is correct, otherwise, your accounts will be linked to erroneous information.

- Credit accounts: reports from banks, financial institutions, and businesses regarding your accounts with them, your credit limit, your balance, and your payment history.

- Credit applications: information about every time a person or organization has requested your credit report in the last 2 years each time you have applied for credit.

- Public records and collections: these are local records of your bankruptcies, annexes, lawsuits, wage garnishments, property liens, and judgments.

Chapter 4: Credit Card

We all want to buy a credit card, or we already have one in our possession, but what is credit? What do we call a credit card? By credit, we must understand that it is a financial operation in which an amount of money is made available to us up to a specified limit and during a set period of time. It's a present right to future payment. Credit is trust; in business, it is the trust given or taken in exchange for money, goods or services.

In the case of the so-called credit card, this is issued by the bank of your choice, allowing multiple transactions in different establishments that use the brand of the card. By obtaining one, it allows us to speed up the forms of payment for any type of product that we need or want, can be both national and international as long as the brands associated with your credit card are leading payment brands in the world.

The credit cards are made of a very resistant plastic material, in addition to having security measures that guarantee their validity such as the relevant identification, the magnetic stripe and even the chip that was incorporated into the cards obligatorily a few years ago as a preventive measure in case of cloning, theft or fraud of the same.

The credit cards are used as an option of payment in many occasions, but this one should not replace the traditional forms of payment as it is it the cash, nor much less to be used of unrestrained form, since as we use the available line of credit it will become a debt to pay, that will be able to be collected of direct form or in installments, this according to the percentage value of the rate of interest of purchases emitted according to the tariff of the bank. It is very important to know that shopping interest rates are very different from cash withdrawal interest rates, that only some cards usually have this option.

You must be very aware that credit cards are not salary extensions or additional money, they are a method of payment that provides benefits and like any financial instrument, has a cost and a high responsibility that must be assumed by the cardholder. The secret of success is to have a clear debt capacity. For many, plastic is the beginning of their credit life, so keeping a good record (making smart use of your credit) is important to their work, family and financial lives.

The best and most responsible way to use a card is to have knowledge of several important points when you acquire or plan to have one:

- Know the billing cycle:

When making an evaluation to acquire a credit card, the bank official has the duty to ask you the days in which you have economic solvency, that is to say, you have the possibility to make the payments corresponding to the debt that you have accumulated using the card and according to it advise you to know which day will be your date of invoicing and an approximate of your next dates of payment.

- Know your credit card rates:

Depending on the type of card and category you have, depending on your financial solvency, you will need to know the annual and monthly interest rates. This will serve as a guide, to know if you will place your purchase directly or in installments.

It is advisable, not to place low amounts or easy to pay in installments, since for each installment a monthly interest is generated, that at the end of accounts the value of the acquired product costs you the double. Also, to know that if you place a product with the commitment to pay it directly or in a single installment, this means, without generating any interest. You will have to pay it on the agreed date because otherwise, you will incur in arrears, this interest will generate deferred interest which, according to the tariff, may be higher than the interest rate of purchases.

- To know the amount of the penalty in case of default:

When you default on the payment date, interest will be added according to the bank in which you belong, since this is usually a percentage of the minimum quota, having a range of the minimum and maximum amount to be charged.

- Know the annual membership to pay or the minimum consumption amount for the exoneration:

Some credit cards do not charge annual membership, but others do, in this case, you should know with what amount you can avoid paying the membership, which can be considered as payment for using the brand of the card and its various benefits it brings with it, always consider the type of plan and service are those you need when acquiring a credit card best suited to your pace of life.

- To know the tax-deductible insurance that banks charge monthly on a mandatory basis:

This is only in the event of death or any accident or illness that makes it impossible for you to carry out the basic or work functions that allow you to support yourself financially, i.e. when you cannot generate income to cancel your payments, a direct relative may request information from the bank about the tax deduction insurance and how to exercise it, in order to assume the expenses of the person holding the credit card.

- Keep track of credit card expenses:

You can do this by having your account statements printed out or by using an Excel spreadsheet. If you receive your EECC by email, we often receive so much information that we cannot see the EECC on time, it is usually also the most economical way, because the shipment has an extra cost, but what can be considered to avoid this, is to have a scheduled date to print or make the Excel table. This should be considered about 5 days after your billing date because the day you bill your card is the day the bank will collect your purchases at your EECC and specify it in the system.

- Don't overshoot:

Keep in mind that some credit cards have the option of being overdrawn, to know more detail of it, you must know your available credit line and have control of your expenses. The overdraft can sometimes save you when you don't have enough money to be able to buy something, but then in your EECC, you will be able to see the charge for it and the interest charged by the entity.

- Don't spend more than you earn:

Despite the fact that you place the consumption in installments, you have already used a large amount of your credit line and in case of an emergency, you will not have the economic solvency to pay the full amount invoiced in your card and the emergency. And if you did, the next month it could happen again and you'd be in a never-ending cycle of debt.

According to these points already exposed, one can have an order when buying a product with a credit card, however we must not only consider it, but we must be very careful with the use of this plastic so well known by fraudsters.

Usually, the main security measures you should have are the following:

- Only the credit card holder should know the PIN for cash withdrawals or when requested to do so by an establishment.

- Do not lose sight of your credit card, as it is enough to know your full details, the expiration date of the card and security code to be able to make an online purchase in a store or register it in an application.

- If your card gets lost, it's a good idea to block it immediately, even though it's just a loss, a credit card in the wrong hands can make endless purchases in minutes.

- If you visualize in your EECC a consumption that you don't recognize, you must block your card and issue a claim for unrecognized consumptions to the bank, according to the estimated term for a claim, they will carry out the verifications and they will send you a notification or letter of answer, giving to know the detail of the consumption and answer of the case, of not being satisfied with the answer issued by the bank, you can make an appeal.

- To deactivate the option of purchases by the Internet of your credit card, this prevents that although they know third people your data and information of your card, the same system of the bank prevents that the purchases are made. The only person authorized to activate this option is the holder and with the appropriate recognition measures to do so.

- To deactivate the option of purchases and use in the exterior of your credit card, as the previous point this option will allow you to have more security. It is recommended that if you travel, you activate it with exact dates and mentions that register the countries in which you will use the card.

TYPES OF CREDIT CARDS

There are several types of credit cards, starting with the world's leading payment brands, as they are:

- Visa

- Mastercard

- American Express

- Diners Club

And also, according to the category of credit card you acquire, according to your monthly income, the most common are:

- Classic

- Gold

- Platinum

- Signature

- Infinite

But as demand for these cards grew, each leading payment brand created new versions of these card categories, being unique and with different features and benefits.

Chapter 5: How to get a credit card?

Some financial institutions require that the person who wishes to acquire a credit card have a passive account with them, that is, a savings account, salary account or a fixed-term deposit. It is worth mentioning that this is not a requirement, but it helps the financial institution to have prior knowledge of your income and can facilitate the acquisition of a card. The requirements to be able to obtain one, are depending on what is requested by the bank, but next the most essential will be announced.

- Coming of age

In some cases, some banks request an exact age to acquire a credit card.

- Have economic solvency:

You must show that you generate monthly income and that you do not exceed your capacity for over-indebtedness. You can attach your pay stubs, receipts for fees or other means to support your economy. The more years they have worked in a company, the lower the risk for the bank, which helps in the credit evaluation.

- Have a good credit history:

If you are a person who has had a credit card before and has been late in their payments for about 4 to 6 months, let me tell you, you do not have a good credit history and it will be very complicated to get a credit card, because of the risk that represents. But if you are a person who is just beginning with the banking and getting his first card, in good time, you have the proper tips to avoid being reported in the central risk.

- Have an Aval:

If you are with a bad category in the central risk, but you paid all your debt with that financial institution and the system is still not updated. You may be asked for a guarantee and your letter of no debt, as collateral for the loan to be given.

These are only some of the requirements that banks request, however it will depend on the credit evaluation that they make, analyzing many more points.

Chapter 6: Advantages and Disadvantages of Credit Cards

The use of credit cards is constantly increasing, but there are still many people who are against them and others who simply don't care about a credit card, but is it good to have a credit card? How convenient is it to go through life without one?

However, credit cards are also one of the easiest ways to get goods and services instantly and in case we run out of cash, as well as providing unique benefits you won't find in other types or forms of payment (such as debit or cash).

Due to the demand for credit cards in the world, the benefits they provide to people have increased. Many of these allow us to live more pleasurable experiences and save money, as well as being a safer method of payment than carrying cash.

Like any credit, cards have their advantages and disadvantages, and, to a great extent, their convenience depends on the particular needs and lifestyle of each person, so I will point out some of the main advantages and in the same way disadvantages you may have for the use of credit cards.

Advantages:

- You won't have huge amounts of cash in your wallet anymore, nor will you run the risk of losing your savings on that product you wanted to buy so much.

- You have a wide range of services that you can cover with the credit system. To make hotel reservations or rent a car is almost essential to have a credit card, as it acts as a guarantee. Again, the card is not necessarily a form of financing, but a pass to access services as simple as those mentioned above.

- Immediate liquidity whenever you need it. If you use credit responsibly, a card guarantees that you will have money available when you need it.

- You can defer the value of monthly purchases with or without interest, this way you can plan your expenses according to your income and thus decide which payments to make with your income and which will be paid with the bank credit of your card.

- You have the possibility of extending credit cards to your relatives or associates for greater control of expenses.

- You can access the cash advance in times of hardship. Unfortunately, not all the loans on the market are so fast, sometimes you have to wait days for them to resolve, and in case of an emergency, that's not an option.

- Security against theft.

If your wallet is stolen or lost, there's no way to recover the cash you had in your wallet. However, one phone call to cancel your cards is enough to prevent someone else from spending your money. Also, banks offer fraud insurance to back you up if your card is used without your authorization. This is also a benefit you can get by using debit cards instead of cash.

- Online purchases are instantly eligible.

The Internet has opened the doors to practically any type of commerce with just a few clicks. Although today there are more and more online stores that allow you to make your payments in convenience stores or bank deposits, it is much faster and more convenient to buy and pay from the comfort of your home, from the super home to the shoes you loved on the other side of the world. Also, you can also pay for your services (water, electricity, telephone, internet, etc.) through the internet, or by direct debit so that they are automatically charged to your card. So, instead of worrying about the date and amount of payment for each service, you only pay for your card.

- Access to exclusive promotions, you have probably seen promotions that are valid only with a credit card.

The use of a card does not always go hand in hand with a lack of liquidity. Even if you have the money to make a cash payment you can use a credit card to get discounts or other promotions; you don't even have to get into debt, once you've made the promotion valid you can immediately pay off your credit card with the money you already have if that worries you. Rewards programs: points and miles, when you make practically any payment with your credit card, you accumulate points that, depending on your bank's promotions, you can use to buy products, flights, travel, obtain discounts or make payments in some establishments, an advantage that no other form of payment offers you. If you simply change your form of payment from debit or cash to credit (without even spending more than necessary) you'll already be making a profit.

- Create a credit history, foresee future needs.

Maybe at this moment you don't need a credit card to finance your purchases or you are not interested in the immediate benefits like all the ones we already mentioned, but the good long-term management of your credit card will allow you to create a credit history, which is in many cases indispensable for you to obtain large credits such as mortgages, automobiles or business. Even if today is not part of your plans, maybe tomorrow you will need them.

- Access large purchases on deferred payments without affecting your monthly expenses.

What happens when you suddenly need a new refrigerator or computer? There are thousands of low-cost used product options but what if you want a new one? If you don't have savings, you will probably have to use the credit offered by the store, that of small weekly payments that take years to pay off and with high-interest rates. If you have a credit card, you will probably find promotions of payments to months without interests so that you neither have to make a great disbursement that you did not have planned nor do you have to pay interests for your financing.

Disadvantages:

- You buy more on impulse. He's tempted to buy with the money that doesn't exist in his bank account.

- More interest is paid, depending on the number of installments to which a purchase is deferred.

- High-interest rates or many countries with no fixed term.

- Fees for handling plastic.

- If your credit history is impoverished due to delinquency, your quality of life will be affected by not being able to access future credit plans, which in turn impedes your goal of obtaining a mortgage, an auto loan, or even medical coverage.

Of course, all the above points will depend on the good use or misuse you give your credit card and of course, the simple fact of having a credit card implies that you must have a fixed monthly income or some income that serves as a support to have financial resources to cover the commitments made.

As you can see, a credit card has great benefits, whether you use it regularly for your everyday expenses or it's a backup in case of emergencies. It is also important to consider that if you are asked for credit history and you still don't have one, remember that the use of a credit card can help you build one.

If after reading this you decide to test your benefits to see if it is good to have a credit card remember that the key, in addition to being responsible for your payments, is to compare different cards from different banks, their costs, and benefits to choosing the one that suits you best.

Chapter 7: How to overcome credit card debt?

Now, if you already have your credit cards and you have incurred expenses greater than your income, of course, the monthly payments will be difficult to cover without affecting the budget necessary for the maintenance of your basic expenses such as variable expenses which are vital to your livelihood. It is at this point that you will require the design of a plan to get out of the debts that afflict you so that it does not affect your requirements and you can recover your credit history.

In that sense, you can consider the following suggestions if you want to get out of your credit card debt:

1. You should suspend the use of credit cards, especially those that demand higher interest payments. Do not hesitate to use scissors to cut them for safety and freedom is better not to have what is not going to be used.

2. Of course, you should not stop paying the monthly installment of your credit cards and if necessary, to achieve this end go to the financial and banking agencies to request the renegotiation of the debt being able to agree on monthly payments that can amortize the debt.

3. If you have extensions of your credit card you must eliminate the temporary or definitive use of those credit cards to your relatives or associates, all will benefit above all your credit history.

4. You must give priority to your expenses and if necessary, for your job only allows you to have the credit cards that yield greater benefits and you can get offers in cases of having to travel exclusively for work.

5. Since you cannot finance your card payments on time and your income does not allow it, opt for alternative jobs that allow you to earn new income. Don't make the mistake of incurring new debts to pay the one you already have.

6. The sumptuous and leisure or recreation expenses that you usually add to the credit on your cards should be suspended for the duration of the credit recovery or payment of delinquent debts.

7. At the moment of undertaking again the use of the credit cards investigate and inform yourself properly of the interest rate, the taxes that require and use those that are of your utility, at this point always less is more.

The commitment you make to your credit history is yours alone and your responsibility, so don't think that there will be magic solutions to get you out of the excesses committed.

Final recommendations:

- Remember, the recovery of your credit history will depend on the degree of commitment you have, controlling your finances. You must program your expenses making a budget where you can, according to your income, distribute the payments of your expenses.

- If you delegate this function you will not change your consumption habits and therefore you will continue with uncontrolled expenses that put you at risk and prevent you from recovering your credit history. Above all, don't pay a credit repair agency to do work that is solely your responsibility, and these agencies often use illegal or unreliable tactics. Maybe you could end up having more problems than benefits.

- You should be aware of the due dates of your payments, take into account that even if you pay your debts in full every month, your account statement could still show that you owe a certain amount. So, pay attention to the deadlines that have been set and in which you must make payments and do so before the statement is sent to you.

- Limit the use and opening of accounts in stores as this negatively affects your credit rating in the short, medium and long term. Uses only credit cards obtained at financial and banking agencies of wide credibility. Also, consider not using more than one-third of your line of credit unless you're sure you can afford to pay it in full that same month. Do not leave debts for the next few months, thinking that you will be able to pay it with an income that is not fixed.

- Many companies pretend to offer free credit reports but charge for their monitoring services. These companies encourage you to sign up for a free report, ask for your credit card and automatically switch you to a paid service after a trial period. Therefore, if you do not cancel your subscription within this period, you will be charged every month for their services.

- If you need specific information about local credit reporting agencies or other aspects of credit ratings where you live, check with the relevant agencies in your country.

- The financial reality is going to be changing in each country and of course the economic conditions in some countries can sometimes be unfavorable especially for micro and small business entrepreneurs, as they cannot access bank loans, are forced to resort to informal lenders, weakening their financial and economic capacity, because the interest rates they charge tend to rise steadily, often exceeding the rates of return generated by their businesses, and instead of helping to grow, often ended up decapitalizing them. In the face of this, it is preferable to turn to trusted individuals or state entities for credit support or refinancing.

How to Raise your Credit Score: Volume 2

Proven Strategies to Repair Your Credit Score, Increase Your Credit Score, Overcome Credit Card Debt and Increase Your Credit Limit

By

Income Mastery

Chapter 1: Credit History

What is a credit history?

Your credit history shows how you've managed your finances and paid off your debts over time. Your personal credit report is a list of information in your credit history that begins the first time you apply for credit. From that point on, each time you apply for a credit card or loan, the information will be added to your credit history. The most important component of your credit report is whether you make your payments on time.

To predict your financial future, many companies look at your credit history through your credit report. A credit history is a profile within a credit report that shows how a person handled their money in the past.

It may include information such as:

- How quickly have you paid off credit cards and loans?

- How reliably have you paid other bills, such as rent and utilities?

- Your total outstanding debts.

- Your credit is available on mortgages, bank cards, auto loans and other lines of credit.

Credit history is a key determinant of who can and cannot get ahead financially. While it was originally intended to be used by lenders to evaluate whether or not a consumer is approved for new credit, credit history is currently used for many non-credit purposes. Although credit reports can be a good source of information regarding loan repayment and loan history, there are few links between your credit history and some of your most recent applications, such as getting a job, renting a home, or obtaining health insurance.

Not having a credit history can lead to lost opportunities; credit history is now often used as a filter for a variety of non-credit purposes; this includes housing, employment, insurance rates, utilities, security clearances and insured health services. This can lead to a significant loss of wealth creation opportunities, along with an increase in wealth depleting events such as increased use of alternative financial services or health-related debt. Many employers use credit history as a way to evaluate potential employees. The Society for Human Resource Management found 47% of employers perform credit checks on job applicants. A wide range of positions, from high-level financial positions to maintenance work may require a credit check. Employers can eliminate applicants with credit problems from hiring even though there is no evidence of a link between poor credit and poor job performance.

In good credit plays an important role in your financial life. Not only is it essential to qualify for a loan or get a credit card, but also to get cell phone service, rent a car and maybe even get a job.

A short credit history can have a negative impact on your score, but a short history can be offset by other factors, such as timely payments and low balances.

Information about your credit history is routinely collected by organizations called credit bureaus. Each credit bureau has its own collection of data about each person, which generally includes personal information, collections of information, information from public records, and information about payment history and outstanding debts. Taken together, all this information about you becomes your credit history.

Influencing Factors

Many factors are used to analyze your credit history:

- Your payment history.

- The amount owed.

- Credit usage time.

- How often do you apply for new credit and assume new debt?

- The types of credit you currently use, such as credit cards, retail accounts, installment loans, finance company accounts, and mortgages.

It is important to keep in mind that your income level is not a factor considered when analyzing your credit history. Someone with a high-income level, for example, may have a low credit score, while someone with a low income level may have a high credit score. It all depends on the use of credit and the factors described above.

Importance

A good credit history increases the confidence of those in a position to lend you money, such as lenders and creditors. When they see that you've paid off your loan as agreed, lenders are more likely to give you credit again. You're going to be seen as a person who fulfills his agreement. With good credit, you can borrow for future major expenses, such as a car, home or education, and you can borrow money at a lower cost.

Generally speaking, the better your credit, the lower the cost of obtaining that credit usually in the form of interest rates and fees. That means you'll have more availability for savings and expense. Lenders will have more confidence in your ability and commitment to repay the loan on time and in full.

However, if your credit history is not strong, you will have to pay higher interest rates, fees, and have less chance of getting money for savings and expenses. Over time, higher rates and fees translate into the loss of thousands of dollars of potential savings.

The rate you will pay for a loan is usually determined by your credit report and credit score. Lenders typically provide "A" loans for people with good, excellent credit, or who have made payments as agreed over the past 24 months. These loans generally have the lowest interest rate. Lenders rate "B" or "C," or "high-risk" loans for people with past or current credit problems, as late payments. These loans generally have higher interest rates.

What is a credit?

Credit is an agreement made with a company or individual to receive goods, products or services that will be paid for in the future. It is a measure of your financial reliability and can be used for small or large purchases. Loans, which are often credit-based and involve borrowed money that has to be repaid in this case with interest.

Although the word credit often describes a lender's trust in a particular loan, the term also often refers to the particular ways in which this trust allows money to change hands. For example, both credit cards and home mortgages are considered forms of credit.

Types of credits

- Revolving credit allows a consumer to repeatedly borrow up to a predetermined amount for each month, as long as his or her account remains in good standing. This type of credit can be unsecured, as with a credit card, or secured, as with a home equity line of credit, which requires a specific asset to back up your promise to pay. Examples of revolving credit are credit cards and lines of credit.

- Term credit consists of loans that are repaid over time, usually in a series of fixed payments. Examples of this type of credit are: car loans, home mortgages, student loans, personal loans, home improvement loans, and land purchase loans.

Bad credit

For many people to be marked by bad credit risk is like being ostracized by society, the very society that thrives on credit! What a contradiction! Once this bad credit label is awarded to your person, internally the damages are deep.

The problem is exaggerated. This is confirmed by statistics regularly published by federal authorities where nearly 40 to 45 percent of people have bad credit. Once you look at bad credit, doors that were previously open are no longer the same. That's the downside of bad credit.

What a person with bad credit needs to understand is that it's not the end of the world. Those two words only mean that future providers should be careful when dealing with you.

There are a lot of people and companies that know how to repair a bad credit situation. There is a wide range of books available, from the simple to the complex, that at least educate, help people about it, and the various steps that could be taken to overcome it.

If you find yourself in this situation it is because the number of people who have bad credit is also large. While it may not be comforting to be among this group of people, at least you're not alone in it. Self-pity and feeling ashamed doesn't help.

Types of Credit Scores

- Low scores

People with scores ranging from 300 to 549 are considered high-risk borrowers. Having these scores makes it difficult to get approval for lines of credit, loans or financing for a home. If lenders extend your credit to you, it will probably be at high-risk interest rates, which means you'll pay for the risk you pose. This lower score may also be a factor that potential employers will weigh to consider for a new position.

- Mid to high range scores

People with scores ranging from 550 to 649 are moderately high-risk borrowers. Because these scores still have room for improvement, interest rates will remain high and lines of credit low. The national average credit score is about 660. Consumers who consider good investments for lenders are those with scores ranging from 650 to 799. Because bank agencies with these scores have few credit history failures, only payments lost here and there or a high credit index are eligible for competitive interest rates.

- Optimal scores

People with scores ranging from 800 to 850 are an excellent investment for lenders. Borrowers in this range can get a loan, buy a car or finance a home with ease. They are eligible for the lowest interest rates available. Once people use the credit they have earned, it is important that they continue to maintain good habits, especially as simple access to large sums of money carries greater responsibility.

Chapter 2: How to Repair Your Credit History?

The use of credit cards sometimes causes problems for people. This may be due to supervision or other financial problems or emergencies that may get in the way of credit card payments. It's pretty simple to repair a credit history, it takes some time and a little work to repair bad credit.

The bad credit situation is the worst situation in life, this not only hinders your current life, but also affects your future prospect of getting a loan.

Whether or not you were a good credit risk in the past, this is considered to be the best indicator of how you will react to debt in the future. For this reason, late payments, loan defaults, tax defaults, bankruptcies and other unsatisfied debt liabilities will count against you even more. Not much can be done about your financial past, but starting today to pay your bills on time can help you increase your credit score in the future.

Factors Leading to Poor Credit Situation

There's no single reason to get into a bad credit rating. Some of the root causes of this are as follows:

- Overspending is the most crucial factor leading to a bad credit history.

- Different unavoidable situations such as health problems, unemployment and other financial problems also have an impact on a credit history.

- Failure to pay on time also affects your credit history.

Types of Credit Repair

Credit Repair Through Debt Consolidation

Although everyone's economic status and situation are different, almost everyone has been in some way in debt at any given time. This can mean small debts such as credit card bills or in-store financing, as well as larger, outstanding loans and mortgages. What this means is that almost everyone depends on being allowed a certain amount of credit, and without credit many of the things you take for granted will become difficult. Once a default is evident, or you fail to make a payment to the credit bureaus, your credit bureau will receive a notice and you will find yourself with a poor credit rating. Effective credit repair involves many different steps and is particular to each individual's situation. A good solution for most people in terms of credit repair is debt consolidation.

One of the most important things in credit repair is to act quickly. Although your credit score will be damaged as soon as you start losing payments to your creditors, you'll get worse if you continue to do so. Many people get confused about whether having credit is good or bad and once they are in trouble with a creditor it is useless to try to rectify it. However, the opposite is true, so even if you are in bad shape with creditors, repair requires them to pay their debts as quickly as possible.

The problem, of course, is that you probably don't have the money to pay the debts, after all, your financial situation was probably the reason for the late payments. For this reason, debt consolidation can be an excellent tool in credit repair. It works by consolidating all your debts into one loan. In other words, if you have multiple outstanding debts, you take a loan from a company, use that loan to pay the debts, and then make payments only on this new loan.

Debt consolidation allows some flexibility in situations where your debt is becoming unmanageable although ultimately you will owe the same amount of money, you could go into long-term debt, this way your monthly payments would decrease. Most importantly, debt consolidation immediately puts you in a strong position with your creditors, and finally a good omen for credit repair. Things won't be perfect, but your creditors will report that you paid off your debts, so the credit repair process can begin quickly.

Debt consolidation is an important tool in credit repair because it allows your financial status with creditors to change very quickly as you go from someone on bad terms with multiple creditors to someone on good terms with just one. It also allows you to stop damage before things get out of control and gives you the breathing space you need after a credit repair. It is therefore mentioned that this intelligent way of debt consolidation is a valuable tool in credit repair.

Debt Consolidation

A debt consolidation, in other words, is a loan that is taken out to pay off smaller loans, or other types of debt, thus reducing the number of payments made in a month, as well as the amount paid monthly. People under immense debt pressure will often look for a debt consolidation to help ease their monthly obligations.

Benefits

- ✓ All your outstanding debts will be paid.

- ✓ I'd only have one loan to repay.

- ✓ There's a little more income available in your budget.

While a consolidated loan may seem like a good idea, there are disadvantages to being considered before applying for it.

Disadvantages

- ✓ You may pay extra costs in administrative matters.

✓ The interest rate may be lower than your current average debt rate, but in the long run it means you'll pay more in effective interest.

✓ It does not completely eliminate your debt; it is simply the same debt in another form.

Before you sign up for a consolidated loan, calculate how much interest you will pay on your current debt and compare it to the interest you would be paying if you accepted a consolidated debt.

Credit repair through a collection agent

Credit scores are based on your credit report. When banks, credit card companies or any other entity lend you money, they inform an agency of their current status in terms of making their payments on time. The agency then gathers this information into a credit history, which is the best guardian of your credit rating. Negative marks on your credit rating will stay there for 7 years, preventing you from getting higher types of loans.

When you start having late payments to a creditor, whether it's loan or credit card payments or financing payments, the creditor will take several steps in an attempt to get you to pay off your debt. After a series of warnings (usually long), the creditor will eventually sell your debt to a collection company. When a creditor does this, they are effectively "paying off the loan" because they sell the debt to a collection agent at a great discount. Basically, the creditor has decided that their chances of recovering the loan are small enough to be willing to lose as much as half its value to stop pursuing it. When this happens, the creditor will report your credit report to the agency, and you will be left with the lowest possible mark on your credit report, which will affect your score for up to 7 years.

A crucial step in credit repair is to take steps to avoid this "cancellation" of your debt. You should act as soon as possible after being contacted by a collection agent. The first thing you should do is contact your creditor, not the collection company, and see if arrangements can be made to clean up the debt with them. In many cases, if you agree to pay the debt immediately to the creditor, they will remove the "assigned to collections" mark from your credit score, which is essential for rapid credit repair.

If your creditor is unwilling to do this, you are trapped before the collection agency. In terms of credit repair, keep in mind that the mark on your credit score can't get worse right now, the debt has already gone to collections, so take the time to consider all of your options. Generally, the debt collector will contact you aggressively, immediately demanding full payment of the debt, and implies that you will be taken to court if this does not happen.

It is advantageous for you in this situation to understand that the debt collection company has probably purchased your debt at about half its value, so any payment above that will generate a profit for them. Try and offer to pay less than the full value of your debt immediately. In most cases, the collection agent will be motivated to close your file as soon as possible to avoid dragging the process. They will usually be willing to accept a quick payment with a discount so they can move on.

To get the credit repaired as quickly as possible, always try to pay your creditor instead of the collection agent when your debt has gone into collections. If that fails, offer the collection agent a lower figure than the total amount of the loan, full payment should be offered as a last resort.

Credit Repair through Credit Counseling

Like many other things in life, budgeting is a skill, some people are better than others at managing their income and keeping up with their debts. Almost all of us had some kind of debt at a given time like a credit card bill and a pending loan, or a mortgage. By having good debt management, you can maintain a good credit rating that will allow you to continue receiving credit in the future. If you don't make payments on time for your loans, or worse, leave them in default, you'll find yourself with a bad credit history, which will take away many economic opportunities. To perform a credit repair, you must slowly build your credit score again. One thing that can help you do this is seek the help of a credit counselor.

In general, credit counseling is performed by nonprofit agencies, and should not be confused with for-profit credit repair companies. The latter should be avoided. Credit repair companies are known to be scammers, especially those who advertise online. Even if it doesn't turn out to be a scam, a credit repair company probably won't do anything you can't do on your own: they'll tell you to get your credit report and blunt any negative elements and may even suggest that you try illegal activities such as getting a "new" credit score with different data and address.

Conversely, a credit counseling service will only provide counseling. This is the best and smartest way to participate in credit repair. To avoid the above, you must rebuild your credit rating which will be a lengthy process that will require time and discipline. Poor service and a credit counselor will help you make the long-term plans and decisions you need for effective credit repair.

Most good credit counseling organizations will also provide counseling and workshops such as educational materials that will help you learn how to make and stick to a budget, which in the long run will be extremely beneficial to your credit score. They will also be able to provide you with personalized advice, so that you can examine and learn how to improve economic decisions based on your particular credit experience.

The problem with credit repair companies, and the reason you should be suspicious of them, is that they propose a one-size-fits-all solution. Anyone who says they can quickly fix their credit without knowing anything about the situation is not truthful. A credit counselor can be crucial in providing you with exactly the kind of particular attention you need.

Most importantly, if you engage in credit repair using a councilman, your solutions will be long-term, because you will learn to manage your budget more effectively and make permanent changes to your spending habits. This is much better than paying a credit repair company that promises a quick fix that has no educational value to you.

Credit Repair Tips

In today's world, credit is essential. Most of us use credit almost every day without even knowing it: credit cards, car payments, home payments, etc. Unfortunately, most people don't think much about their credit rating until they find themselves in trouble with it. Having a bad credit history affects much more than your ability to get a loan; you'll also have trouble getting all kinds of credit. It is essential to take steps to repair your credit history as quickly as possible. Here are some tips for repairing credit:

- **Get Your Credit Report**

This step is crucial, all credit information is reported by banks and similar credit bureaus, which in turn hold the key to repairing the credit. Most people never consider getting their credit reports until they are trying to repair the credit, but it's always a good idea.

In most cases, there should be no charge for receiving a copy of your credit report; you simply have to request it (usually in writing, in person and accompanied by a copy of your identification). When you are considered a bad creditor for a credit card or loan, the company must indicate which credit bureau reported you as having bad credit, and then you can request a report from that bureau. Credit repair begins with a detailed look at your credit report. Look for any inaccuracies: in some cases, they may be errors in your file, or your credit information may be mistaken for someone else with the same name. Many people are surprised at how often a company reports a late payment in error.

If you find any inaccuracies, you can repair your credit by applying in writing to the credit bureau. If you have any supporting documentation, include it, otherwise simply indicate where the confusion is and request that it be analyzed. This benefits you in two ways: first, if the credit bureau cannot verify the information you are disputing, by default it must be deleted from your file; second, if the bureau does not respond to your request for investigation within 30 days, the disputed information must be deleted.

If it turns out that your bad credit is the result of an error, you should usually go to the credit bureau, that's all you need to do to repair the credit. When you order your credit report, keep in mind that your processors will make the process seem more difficult than it is, since in terms of hours they are not interested in responding to many requests for credit reports.

• Contact your bank agency

Once you have reviewed your credit report and determined that everything is correct, the next step in repairing your credit history is to contact creditors with whom you have delinquent accounts. You should repair these accounts as soon as possible to successfully repair your credit.

In many cases, the creditor's priority is to recover as much of the account receivable as possible. Many people are surprised at how accommodating they can be in terms of organizing a payment process: in many cases, the creditor will eliminate interest or even reduce the bill and return it for immediate payment. If you can't pay immediately, propose a payment plan for the creditor that you can stick to: Creditors will accommodate most payment proposals because, again, your primary interest will be to recover the debt.

Remember that the reason you're doing this is to repair your credit history, so under no circumstances should you commit to a payment plan with your creditors that you won't be able to meet would only end up making problems worse in the future. If a creditor has repeated problems with a client, it is unlikely that there is much trust in the relationship, so they probably won't want to help you. Instead, choose something you can meet and explain your current financial situation to the creditor. By doing this, you can often achieve credit repair fairly quickly.

- **Try and avoid the collection agency**

The worst and last step a creditor will take is to sell your outstanding debt to a collection agency. In terms of credit repair, this is basically the worst thing that can happen because it means that whoever you owed money to consider your chances of recovering it so low that you are willing to lose some of the debt. In most cases, the creditor sells the debt to the collection agency at a large discount, often half the amount owed.

When a debtor sold his loan to a collection agency, he just "canceled" it and created the lowest possible mark on his credit history. If this happens, try and act as soon as possible after being contacted by the collection agent. Before you negotiate with the collection company, talk to your creditor. See if the creditor will remove the "canceled" mark from your credit history. This is something they will do sometimes, in exchange for an immediate payment.

If your creditor is not interested in negotiating payment, you would be in trouble with the collection agent. It can and will happen that the debt collector stays in a very intimidating and threatening position, usually implying that they are willing to take you to trial. The two points to keep in mind is that the collection company bought your debt for less than the amount owed, and you are unlikely to be sued. Your best solution is to offer to make an immediate payment for less than the actual balance of your debt. Most companies will accept this, usually because making a profit on any payment that exceeds 50% of their debt and offering to pay immediately allows them to close their file and work on other issues. When dealing with a collection agent, only offer full payment as a last resort.

• Apply for a secured credit card

Credit repair can be a slow process, and you may find yourself building a bit of credit backing slowly over a long period of time. A good place to start is with a "secured" credit card. These credit cards are issued by banking agencies that generally target people who have bad credit. Unlike a regular credit card, for which you will no doubt be rejected if you have a bad credit, it is a secured credit, the card usually requires you to give an initial deposit equivalent to the credit limit of the card. That is, you give the company $500 for a card with a credit limit of $500, and they reserve the right to use that deposit against any outstanding balance that remains for too long.

From the issuer's point of view, their bad credit won't matter because they don't take any risk: you'll never owe them more money than you've already given them to start with. From your point of view, secured cards are far from ideal, but if you have bad credit and need to participate in credit repair, you have no choice.

Once you have a secured credit card, use it sparingly but regularly and be sure to make all your payments on time. By doing this over a long period of time, you will slowly repair your credit history and regain the confidence of creditors who rejected you in the past.

- **Consider a company that specializes in credit repair**

If you find that none of the above works for you in terms of credit repair, consider going to a company that specializes in this type of process. Many of these companies will offer to "clean up your credit record" for a fee. While the services of a credit repair company can be much more helpful, depending on your situation, you must be very careful to avoid scams and read all the fine print that is in most cases.

The basic strategy of most credit repair companies will be to encourage you to claim absolutely everything on your credit report with your credit bureau. The idea is to flood the office with more requests than they can respond to within 30 days, because remember that if the office can't provide documentation for something in your file within 30 days, it must be remote. However, it is questionable how effective this really is, although the office, if it does not document them, must remove items within 30 days, in most cases companies will continue to investigate the claims, and when they finally find the proper documentation, the items will be added again.

Whatever you decide regarding a credit repair company, always remember to review the documents carefully. Also note that credit repair companies cannot legally accept payments until services are completed. They are also required to clearly describe all payments and terms.

Repairing your credit yourself is the best option

Having a good credit rating is one of the essential tools for leading a successful economic life. Although most people don't think much about their credit history, having good credit allows you to acquire many things that are generally taken for granted: credit cards, car rentals, hassle-free loans, and apartment rentals, and so on. Each time you delay or fail to pay a fee, the creditor will report this to the credit bureau, and it will be added to your credit history. If you do this too often, or let loans fall into default, you will have to perform a credit repair, as you will be consistently rejected for credit cards and most other types of loans.

If you use the Internet or classified ads when you begin your credit repair research, you'll probably notice many offers from companies that offer credit repair services. Most of them aggressively promote themselves and claim that they can fix your credit report quickly for a fee. You should be very cautious when dealing with these companies, many of which are scams, and in most cases, you can repair your own credit more effectively yourself.

It is important to understand that there is nothing a credit repair company can do that you cannot. Do it yourself. In other words, even though it may involve you, a credit repair company is not related to the credit bureau and cannot get low scores on your "erased" credit score so the credit repair company will most likely encourage you to get your credit report from the bureau and challenge negative elements in the report.

In some cases, credit repair companies will even get involved in activities of questionable legality. You will be encouraged to start a "new" credit rating through a change of address and banking information. This practice is not legal, nor is it usually effective. A much better approach to credit repair is to do it yourself. If you search online you will find many sites that offer advice and a step by step, the best option is to follow the advice of a government source or other reliable organization.

The best approach is to first get your credit report from the bank, once you have the report, carefully examine it and claim, written, any errors you may find in the report. Only complain if there are genuine errors, if your report is error-free, you will have to participate in the traditional methods of credit repair. The best way to start is to obtain a secured credit card and use it regularly, this way you will slowly repair your credit score.

By being patient and making smart budget decisions, you'll be able to pay your creditors on time. By doing so, you will eventually prove to them that you are eligible for credit. Although repairing credit in this way is a slow process, it is the only really effective one. With this approach you will have much more long-term success than following a credit repair company.

Chapter 3: Strategies for Increasing Your Credit History

How to establish a good credit history?

The key to establishing a good credit history is to keep your promise to pay off loans or credit cards as agreed, on time and in scheduled amounts, otherwise it will be difficult and expensive to ask for credit for the things you really need for yourself and your family, including a home, education or health care.

Although your intentions may be good, events such as a medical emergency or losing a job may occur, affecting your ability to repay your loans. Therefore, it is essential to set up and regularly contribute to a savings plan because by doing so you may have funds available to meet your credit agreements despite some unforeseen events that may happen in the future.

If you don't currently have credit or rarely borrow money, consider applying for one or two cards to establish credit. Compare and review interest rates and fees, use credit cards carefully, paying off debt each month. It is also important that you keep your overall debt at a reasonable level relative to your income. In general, your expenses should not exceed 20% of your net salary.

Needs versus wants

You can start by thinking about your personal needs and wants. Needs" are items you must have for basic survival, such as food, clothing and shelter. Wishes" are those things you want but can live without, such as fashion items, restaurant meals, or entertainment. Remember, wishes are neither good nor bad. However, you will personally want to balance your needs and desires so that you can successfully establish a savings plan and good spending plan principles. Savings and spending plans will help you establish and maintain good credit and work to establish long-term financial security.

How to make a spending plan?

Establish and maintain a good credit history and demonstrate your ability to manage and pay your debts, make a spending plan and live within it.

To develop a spending plan, you must follow these steps:

1. Determine your monthly income.

2. List your fixed monthly expenses.

3. Know your variable expenses.

4. Track and plan large, recurring expenses.

5. Compare your income with your expenses.

6. Set priorities, goals, and limits.

7. Establish a savings plan and make it a priority.

8. Always maintain an emergency fund.

9. Plan ahead for major purchases and avoid impulse decisions.

Once you are comfortable with a spending plan, you can be more flexible and make adjustments for financial decisions that are in your family's best interest. You use the spending plan which will help you stay within your means.

Improvement strategies

If you want to improve your credit, it is important to understand that no matter what you do, negative events in your credit history will remain there until they are scheduled to expire. Nothing can be done to erase the negative elements, but you can build another solid credit that will help offset the impact of those negative elements, and over time those negative elements may disappear. The key is to take a proactive approach to building credit without overextending yourself. Because your credit history cannot be directly monitored, all you can do is focus on making positive changes that will be reflected in your credit report. Those changes will, over time, be incorporated into your credit history. These are some of the best things you can do to improve your credit history:

1. Pay your bills on time.

One of the most important things you can do to improve your credit history is to pay your bills before the due date and pay the full amount. This means payments on all types of debt, from personal loans to a mortgage for utility bills. You can set up automatic payments from your bank account to help you pay on time, but make sure you have enough money in your account to avoid overdraft fees.

2. If you don't have a credit history, start one.

A long credit history allows you to show consistency and responsibility in your credit management, so the longer your credit history, the better chances you have of getting a high score. If you don't already have a credit history, it's in your best interest to start one, as long as you follow the recommendations described in this section. Make sure you don't open multiple accounts too quickly.

3. Limit your new credit applications.

If you apply for a lot of new loans or lines of credit, it can damage your credit. When you're looking for a loan, it's best to make sure you limit how long you do it. The period of time between your consultations is a way for banks to determine whether you want to buy a single or multiple loan. Viewing your own credit report or score will not harm your credit, nor will creditors reviewing your report or score to make pre-selected bids.

4. If you pay by credit card, pay every month

You will accumulate a line of credit by using your credit card and always paying on time. Pay your statements each month to avoid finance charges.

5. Don't be afraid to talk to your creditors.

Lenders can change your interest rate or reduce your monthly payment. But not if you don't ask.

6. Check your credit regularly.

There is no problem reviewing your credit report on a daily basis. Check for errors or potential fraud.

What if I don't have credit?

Sometimes lenders won't have enough credit references to get you the loan you want. If this is your case, start by opening small lines of credit and making small purchases that can be easily repaid. If you don't already have a checking or savings account, it's best to open one. Your bank can provide you with a credit card once you have established a history with them as a customer.

If you don't have a certain credit, you're not completely out of luck. Some bank agencies have a report that will let them know if people are paying their bills for rent and utilities on time. If they think they're good payers, they can approve a loan. It is therefore extremely important to cancel these daily expenses on time. In addition, your ability to maintain a stable job will improve the likelihood of being approved for credit.

Another option would be to obtain a secured credit card. A secured card can be a great way for a person without credit to establish credit. This type of card works like a debit card and will require deposited funds for purchases, the main difference is that your credit history will be reported at the credit bureaus. However, it is good to do an investigation in advance, and be sure to do so. Also note that not all banks or credit unions offer secured credit cards, some cards may even charge the paperwork and other fees.

It's also a good idea to start saving money for your down payment. The lender will look at your application in the most favorable way when it can provide a 20% down payment. Please note that there are certain loan programs available that allow a percentage of gift money (bonus) for the down payment.

Chapter 4: Credit Cards

How do credit cards work?

Credit cards tend to have higher interest rates than other types of credit, and the rate varies among different types of cards. Interest is charged on all consumptions that remain outstanding for the following month in the event that the (total) amount owed is not paid each month (or within an interest-free period). The interest rate may also be higher if you use the card for cash withdrawal.

How to choose a credit card?

It may be easy to get a credit card at your preferred bank or current credit union, but you may find a better deal elsewhere, so it's best to shop around. Comparison websites can be useful for finding credit card offers.

Interest-free periods vs. credit cards with no interest period

Credit cards with an interest-free period (where you don't pay interest for a certain amount of time after a purchase) often have high annual rates. But if you pay your debt within the interest-free period, you'll avoid paying interest, so the higher rate may be worth it.

On the other hand, if you think you won't be able to pay off your credit card debts every month, it's best to choose a card with no interest days. Generally, you will pay lower annual fees either from the day of purchase or from the day a monthly statement is issued.

Major Credit Card Errors

Credit cards can be a blessing for consumers, as they provide many advantages and benefits because they are an excellent alternative to cash, they are excellent if you need to make purchases when you are in distress. Some cards offer benefits or rewards such as cash back or travel miles, while others provide additional protection for your purchases. If you play your cards right and pay your balances each month, you'll never have to pay a penny in interest. In addition, being a conscious credit card user can help you improve your credit score.

Thousands of consumers have trouble controlling their credit card balances. If you find yourself among these consumers, don't despair. It will make your debt more manageable once you choose to change your spending habits. Take a giant step in this direction by avoiding or stopping making these important credit card mistakes:

- Use of the card for everyday items

One big mistake people often make is using their credit cards for regular, everyday purchases. Except in extenuating circumstances, you should have your budget under sufficient control to pay for your needs with your monthly income. By keeping common purchases such as food supplies and utility bills out of your credit card balance, you'll take an important step toward controlling expenses.

Keep in mind that buying milk with a credit card will eventually become a major expense if you don't pay for your consumption at the end of each month. There is no reason to incur extra interest charges on those necessary items you must purchase directly with monthly income.

- Withdraw cash

Credit card banks use tactics such as mailing messages about cash withdrawals, encouraging you to use them to pay bills or indulge in something good, but rarely make it clear that this money is treated as a cash advance. Taking a cash advance is dangerous because you start earning interest right away, unlike regular credit card purchases. In addition, there is often no grace period and you will be charged an automatic fee that can reach up to 4% on the advance amount. Also, the credit card company may not consider the cash advance to be paid until you have paid off the balance of your other purchases.

- Using the card to pay medical bills

Medical bills can be overwhelmingly expensive, especially if you don't have insurance. If you have trouble paying your medical bills, negotiate an agreement with the hospital or another company you owe money to. Don't increase your bills and stress by adding exorbitant credit card interest rates. You should also review your medical bills a second or third time, making sure they are accurate and that you understand all charges.

- Search for credit card vouchers

Credit card rewards are usually worth far less than the extra interest you'll earn if you can't pay the money you spend to earn those bonds. You may, for example, receive one point for every dollar you spend, but you'll probably need to redeem 5,000 points to get a $100 discount on a plane ticket. Since the interest charged on outstanding account balances often exceeds the typical 2% bonus, it may not be a valuable offset.

You should also avoid subscribing to multiple credit cards, regardless of bonuses. If you already know that you don't manage credit cards well, don't add the temptation in the form of additional cards. It's also easier to miss a payment deadline when you have more cards than you can manage. Remember, some late fees or interest will quickly delay those registration gifts or rewards.

You can use your cards more often once you have paid off your debt and know how to avoid a new debt. As long as you pay your balance in full and on time each month, there's nothing wrong with using credit cards instead of carrying cash or taking advantage of cash back or frequent flyer miles. Just make sure those purchases fit your monthly budget.

- Ignore your debt

Some people are so stressed or embarrassed by credit card debt that they stop extending their accounts and pretend there's no problem. Obviously, it's a bad approach because while ignoring bills, the time bomb of interest rates increases debt. In addition, if you miss one or two payments, the interest rate may skyrocket higher under the terms of the card agreement.

You can call the card companies if you feel overwhelmed and ask to renegotiate the terms of your agreement. You may be able to lower your interest rate, set up a repayment plan or get a share of your debt. If your first call doesn't work, keep calling because a different customer service representative may allow you to negotiate a better deal.

Ignoring debt can also lower your credit score and encourage debt collectors to take action.

- Make minimum payments

Paying the minimum (or even a little more than the minimum) each month on your credit cards may seem like the right thing to do to maintain your credit score, but it's not an effective way to repay the debt.

Given the high interest rates and fees added to what you must pay on credit cards, making minimum payments means that you are only reducing the amount of the original debt. It will take years to pay off your debt this way. In addition, unless you stop using the card, you will continually add new debts as you try to pay off the old ones.

In addition to taking up too much time, this tactic could end up costing you thousands more interest by the time you pay off your debt. That's why it's important to identify if your debt could be a problem and take care of it as soon as possible.

Finally, don't let embarrassment stop you from taking action. You may think everyone else is in control of their finances. However, many of them face debt problems similar to their own.

Reward Schemes

It is important to note that credit cards with special features (such as reward schemes, discounts on certain goods and services, or rebate offers) often have higher interest rates.

Balance Transfer Offers

You can get the full benefit of these offers by paying the transfer amount within the agreed upon period. If the entire amount is not paid before the end of the transfer period, the balance is often charged at the standard interest rate or the cash advance rate (which can be much higher). Terms and conditions may be different for each balance transfer, so make sure you understand what they are.

Chapter 5: How to Overcome a Credit Card Debt?

No matter which debt solution you choose, it's important to start paying off your debts as soon as possible because depending on your creditors, interest on your accounts could increase every day, adding more and more to your debts. Without a solid plan to get out of debt, you could be trapped in an endless cycle of high interest payments that could take years to overcome. That's why it's very important to get out of debt as quickly as possible.

One of the best ways to create a more stable financial future is to overcome debt. Many people are creditors of debt throughout their lives, but if your monthly debt payments are becoming a strong source of stress, it may be time to re-evaluate the way you manage your money.

Steps to Get Out of Credit Card Debt

When you are overwhelmed by credit card debt, or have become accustomed to carrying a balance, it may seem impossible to find a way out. But it can create many paths to a debt-free future. This section will give you six tips on getting out of debt as quickly as possible:

1.   **List all of your debts**

The first step in overcoming debt is to verify the total amount owed. If you have multiple loans, credit card balances and other forms of debt, it is helpful to determine how much you pay each month and which debts are worse than others in terms of general interest rate, minimum monthly payments and more.

Order your debts according to the highest interest rate and total loan balance. What debts are the "worst"? Make a plan to prioritize which debts you will pay first.

2. Track Your Expenses

The next step in getting out of debt is to keep track of how much you spend each month and then find out where you can cut back. Online tools and budgeting software can help you track your spending. Or, if you prefer a more convenient method, simply use paper and pencil or set up a spreadsheet to track your spending for 30 days.

Find out if your bills are fixed expenses or variable expenses: fixed include rent/mortgage, insurance premiums and utilities, while variable expenses include changing expenses, such as groceries, car maintenance. Beyond invoices, how are your discretionary expenses? This could be in things like restaurant meals and entertainment. Once you have this summarized, you can begin to develop strategies to reduce spending in certain areas.

3. Make a "roadmap" to get out of debt

Look for a debt repayment calculator to figure out how much you have to pay each month so you can get out of debt faster. For example, this debt payment calculator will allow you to analyze multiple debt payments, including the total amount, your monthly payment, and interest rates to determine how soon you can be debt free and how much money you will pay in interest along the way.

4. Reduce spending on small items

Once you have a roadmap in mind, it's time to start changing your monthly (and daily) spending habits. Could you save $500 a month by eating less, canceling a gym membership you never use or canceling some subscriptions?

It's worth taking a closer look, many people are surprised to see how much they spend on TV shows they don't watch or premium application subscriptions. By cutting back on small expenses, you can often find a large amount of money to spend on overcoming debt.

5. Reduce Spending on a Big Thing

About small expenses, they help you think big and be ready to make a major change in your monthly budget. How much do you spend each month on renting or paying for your car? You might consider moving to a more affordable place or finding a roommate, if that means getting out of debt sooner.

Don't be afraid to consider making lifestyle changes to get out of debt. Sometimes it is necessary to make a short-term sacrifice to achieve financial stability.

6. Consider ways to earn extra money

Most people think getting out of debt is about spending less. While reducing spending is a good strategy, it's not the only one, you also have the option of doing extra work to earn more money.

Where could you earn extra money? You can get a part-time job, sell some items at a garage sale or in an online marketplace, do a self-employment or increase your income to help you get out of debt. Don't be afraid to think creatively and be willing to work hard in the short term to reach a better financial position.

Methods for Overcoming Credit Card Debts

If all your accounts have a similar interest rate, the Snowball Method might be a better option, but if you have one or two cards with a scandalously high interest rate, the Avalanche Method might be the right solution. It should be noted that both methods require that you have enough money to pay more than the minimum on your credit cards.

Avalanche method

Using this method, people use the extra money they get each month to pay off the debt at the highest interest rate, with all minimum payments remaining. By eliminating higher interest payments faster, you'll pay less interest over the next few months until the total debt is paid off. Once you have paid off your first high interest debt, find the next highest interest rate and repeat the process. Pay above the minimum amount as much as you can, so you can get out of debt faster.

Snowball method

By following this method, people instead of focusing on the highest debt, should first focus on paying off the card with the lowest debt until they reach the largest regardless of the interest rate. Then you work your way so you can pay the most you owe.

Paying debts with the lowest amounts first, you pay off those smaller payments quickly and have fewer bills to worry about. Finally, you should continue to pay the bills with the lowest balances until you have no debt left.

Why is saving so important?

It is important really important to have savings. This will allow you to pay for emergencies, give you financial freedom and it can help you avoid credit problems that could damage your credit score. A high credit score can make it easier to rent an apartment and qualify for new credit.

How do I start saving?

When it comes to saving money, the sooner you start, the better. It is not an act that is accomplished overnight, but it is a process that occurs gradually and grows over time. Making ends meet can be a challenge and you'll wonder how you can save on everything, but any amount saved is progress. As you get into the habit of saving routinely you will see that the money saved is increasing.

Contact your credit provider and make a payment plan

You can visit your creditors in person or call them on the phone and try to negotiate easier payment terms.

Creditors are usually open to negotiating easier payment terms if you are in a tight position can indicate the figure you can pay and increase the payments to your measure so that they can be paid.

- Act early: try your account before it's too late. It is easier and cheaper to deal directly with creditors than with debt collection agencies.

- Be honest and polite: explain your current financial position. You don't have to go into details, but a little explanation should be enough.

- Understand what you will get: how will the interest charged under the new payment agreement be? What is the final amount you will have paid at the end of the term Don't be afraid to ask questions?

- Take notes: be sure to get a reference number and name for any questions you may have.

- Always ask for evidence in writing: whether it's a confirmation email or a statement about the company on letterhead, for your own protection you need to make sure you have something in writing that confirms the new arrangement.

Bibliography

McKenna, J. Makela, C. y Porter, N. (2014). Informes crediticios. Recuperado de https://mountainscholar.org/bitstream/handle/10217/195073/AEXT_091412014-spa.pdf?sequence=1&isAllowed=y

De La Madrid, R. (2012). Reports on discrimination in Mexico 2012. Retrieved from https://www.conapred.org.mx/userfiles/files/Reporte%20D-CREDITO-Web_INACCSS.pdf

Vladilo, V. (2011) Credit Peace: Learn how to repair, obtain, or improve your credit. Retrieved from https://s3.eu-west-1.amazonaws.com/eu.storage.safecreative.org/1/2011/05/27/00000130/332b/da11/8f5f/89944ea89a6b/PAZCREDITICIACONBONOparaimprimir.pdf?response-content-type=application%2Fpdf&X-Amz-Algorithm=AWS4-HMAC-SHA256&X-Amz-Date=20191017T044116Z&X-Amz-SignedHeaders=host&X-Amz-Expires=86400&.X-Amz-Credential=1SXTY4DXG6BJ3G4DXHR2%2F20191017%2Feu-west-1%2Fs3%2Faws4_request&X-Amz-Signature=39ff7d233d54b90f183d3f615891f617cf0350afa9fbaea5565f16348278eb44

Molina, V. (2002) El Gestor de cobranza. Retrieved from
https://books.google.com.pe/books?id=Id37m
ei83AICg=PA30q=creditos+y+cobranzas&hl=
en&sa=X&ved=0ahUKEwjR75fTv6LlAhVCi1
kKHYkdDQcQ6AEINjAC#v=onepage&q=cr
edits%20y%20cobranzas&f=false

Pimenta, C. and Pessoa, M.(2015). Gestión Financiera
publica en América Latina: la clave de la
eficiencia y la transparencia. Retrieved from
https://books.google.com.pe/books?id=1bF2
DwAAQBAJrintsec=frontcoverq=la+key+of+
efficiency+and+transparency&hl=en&sa=X&v
ed=0ahUKEwjp68isv6LlAhWGwFkKHatEDU
MQ6wEIKjAA#v=onepage&q=la%20key%20
of%20la%20efficiency%20y%20transparency&f
=false

Panasiuk, A. (2003). How do I get out of my debts? .
Retrieved   from
https://books.google.com.pe/books?id=4p_t6
kuaMOUCrintsec=frontcoverq=deudasl=esa=
Xed=0ahUKEwi11f6LwaLlAhUJvVkKHWGo
ACMQ6AEIKDAA#v=onepage=deudas=false

How to Raise your Credit Score: Volume 3

Proven Strategies to Repair Your Credit Score, Increase Your Credit Score, Overcome Credit Card Debt and Increase Your Credit Limit

By

Income Mastery

Chapter 1. Knowing the Credit History

1.1. A mistake I made while using a credit.

I must confess that it was a dark chapter in my life regarding the economy, which I handled very badly. In August 2016, I exceeded the credit card usage of a well-known bank in some countries Let's move on. I generated a debt equivalent to $350. Then, I continued to hinder my credit history by paying the minimum amount, which was about $290; every month, because at that time I was earning almost $475 a month. If I paid off my debt in full, I would have about $85 left to live in the month and in transportation it was at least $59 a month.

I wouldn't be able to afford food, housing or services. At the time I was living in a room near my work center. I had to go out on commissions and the consultancy lasted four months, without contemplating payments for gratification, medical breaks or other inclusions that I could earn as a collaborator of the company in which I worked. In December of that year my consulting ended, but I was still paying the minimum of that $290 debt.

At the beginning of 2017 I was already stuck with debt, when a friend paid what I owed to the bank. However, my job at the time did not allow me to pay her back, since she earned a minimum wage of $267. She was fired at the end of 2018; that's when I began to pay her, with an exchange: she took out a $295 credit, distributed over two years. She paid for the first year until she was fired from her job. So, I assumed the debt until the end of the second year of it.

There are many lessons for me and for you: don't overdraft credit cards, don't spend more than you earn and don't pay the minimum amount indicated on the credit card because it generates more debt. All because I didn't know whether or not I should overdraft my card, and whether or not I had the ability to pay that debt.

Here's the reference to what you shouldn't do in your credit history. What comes next are the concepts and indications of what you will do to avoid falling into debt, like me.

1.2. Financing of appropriations

To begin with, credit is a key tool in our finances; learning to manage it properly will help you achieve your goals and objectives. Analyze several factors of your financial situation before asking for a credit: how many debts you have, what are your fixed expenses and with which assets you have. Here the various types of credits:

1.2.1. Revolving credit. *Revolving credit* is a type of credit that does not have a fixed number of installments, in contrast to conventional credit. Examples are those associated with credit cards that provide a line of credit on which purchases and payments are made. A revolving credit allows you to dispose of the money that you do not have at the moment, but that you will receive in the immediate future. It has a cut-off date, which establishes the beginning and end of a period of purchases and payments; and a payment date, which is the last day to pay, so the bank will consider you and not penalize you.

Other types of cards are the credit cards of stores or supermarkets, which are used to buy in their establishments. With both you can take advantage of monthly promotions, no interest and other additional benefits. Before applying for a card, always review the total annual cost, interest rate, commissions, promotions and other benefits, as well as other terms and conditions. For example, when I acquired my first credit card I was able to buy my first laptop, taking advantage of a promotion at the moment.

1.2.2. Loans of free investment or personal. These are open credits that, when you apply for them, you do not have to explain how you will use them, and they can also be fragmented. They are offered by banks, financial institutions and even companies dedicated exclusively to offer them. Make sure it is a serious company and check the stipulations of your contract before signing. Always consult, compare and review the total annual cost, annuity, commissions, as well as all terms and conditions.

It also draws up your budget and verifies your ability to pay. A personal example I cite is that this type of credit was used by my parents for home remodeling, and another for a trip. In my case, I was offered a loan of about $2900, but I declined other occupations and more primary payments. Benefits? Several, in addition to the possibility of achieving a good credit history: no paperwork (only with your identity document) and access in less time than a regular application. With a free investment loan you have up to 60 days grace period to pay the first instalment. You will also be able to pay in the instalments that are most convenient for you.

1.2.3. Specific appropriations. This is the credit, the amount of which can only be used for one purpose, and you must check that you used it for that purpose. Your advantage is in the amounts and payment plans that are designed according to the objective. These credits are, for example, mortgage, educational and automotive, among others. An example of this type of credit are the loans granted by the universities, once the educational career is over and more a job from the same university. These loans must be repaid at a certain time, up to a maximum of 10 years.

Of course, some of the conditions that the university requires of the student must be met, such as taking an undergraduate course and positioning oneself in the upper third as one of the best students of the faculty, in addition to being placed in the medium and high pension scales of the university. These scales are associated with pension systems that students pay according to their economic situation. There are houses of studies that contemplate nine levels, being the first the lowest and the ninth the highest. Another example are the educational credits provided by various banks, whose payment period is usually shorter (five years) and the amount to lend the equivalent of $30000, and involve payment facilities.

1.2.4. Consumer Durable Goods Loan. This type of credit is related to the acquisition of goods that have a commercial value and a certain useful life, such as automobiles, computer equipment, household appliances, furniture and equipment. The borrower must contribute a percentage of the total cost and the bank lends the rest. These assets can sometimes serve as collateral for the loan.

For example, when someone close to my circle of friends applied for a loan to buy a dozen computers and explained to the financier that this loan was to set up an Internet cyber, in which he invested his savings. With this he guaranteed that the financial company would lend him the monetary amount to finalize the purchase of the equipment. Once this was done, my colleague began to pay the installments corresponding to his loans, while his business progressed. It had to receive shortly the visit of the collaborators of the financier, who photographed the environments of the cyber, and the equipment. My friend had to sign the compliance papers.

1.3. Simple but important terms for dealing with credit history

1.3.1. Debt capacity. Also called credit use, ability to pay, or debt ratio. A measure related to how much debt you have on your card versus how much you are allowed to spend. According to experts consulted by a bank in some countries, the borrowing capacity limit is between 35% and 40% of the monthly net income. The result of the subtraction of total revenues and fixed expenses in a month.

Let's do this exercise: add up all your income and then subtract all the payments you have to make. The remaining money, which is "free," represents what you could put into the loan each month.

A credit card with $900 of debt and a credit limit of $1000 has a very high debt ratio: 90%.

1.3.2. Annual Effective Cost Rate (AECR). It is composed of the interest rate, but also of additional costs for arrears, physical account shipments, among others. This extra amount for services varies according to the bank. For example, some credit cards in some countries have a TCEA of 104.04% while others have 124.55%, and some figures close to 154.7%.

1.3.3. Wildcard quota. It is one of the benefits given by some banks. In some cases, you may be given the option to access it once a year, twice during the entire loan, depending on the bank. Necessarily, you have to be punctual in your payments. Take into account that this is not a saving, but postponing the payment, because they set the new schedule of payments, because the interest continues.

1.3.4. Value Added Tax (VAT). Also known as Value Added Tax. It is an indirect tax on consumption levied on the supply of goods and services. It is not applied directly to the income of taxpayers, but is paid according to the consumption made by each person. The more products or services you buy, the more VAT you pay. It is the same rate for everyone, regardless of the income of the taxpayer from whom the tax is being levied. It is proportional and deals with a certain percentage that applies to all products and services. In most countries there are two, three and up to four VAT rates, depending on the product or service to which the tax is subject. Find out about VAT in your country.

Chapter 2. Credit History, Here We Go!

2.1. What is a credit history?

According to Oscar Salas, former Director of Product and Business at Afluenta, fintech of collaborative finance in Argentina: The credit history is elaborated with data provided by financial institutions as well as telephone, electric, automobile, or insurance companies. This qualification will be the one that will allow you to obtain credit.

2.2. How can I get my credit history?

Start by getting a cell phone plan, a department store card, or cable TV. Another way is to apply for a credit card; when you start using it, you'll enter your credit history. Also, get a loan from your trusted financial institution. A financial product such as a savings account is also an option for obtaining credit history.

My brother, a graphic designer by profession, contracted Internet service with fixed telephony when he was 19 years old; this is how he entered the world of credit history. Another example is the opening of my first credit card when I was working as a communications consultant for an international organization. I had certified that I had been working there for a long time, so that I could be issued the card. Previously, he was an intern for another company; although he had monthly payments, he was not subject to credit.

2.3. What is a credit rating?

It is a score given by measurement agencies to the credits or debts of different companies, governments or individuals, depending on their credit quality. It is based on the credit history of a natural or legal person and, above all, the ability to repay the financing. This capacity is based on the analysis of all the liabilities and assets of the subject to be evaluated. Credit ratings range from 300 to 850. A low rating indicates lower creditworthiness and a high rating indicates higher creditworthiness. Most financial professionals recommend a credit rating of at least 700. Ratings equal to or above 700 allow a borrower to earn lower interest rates on loans and credit cards than others with lower credit ratings.

2.4. This is how I ruin my credit history

You begin to have a bad record of not paying your credit card bills on time, as I did at the beginning of this chapter. Another way is to fail someone who presented himself as your guarantor to the bank and did not pay on time. How many relatives and friends presented themselves as guarantors for their acquaintance to pay the credit and, in the end, they were the ones who had to pay a debt that was not their own, because the subject could not pay the outstanding bills.

Similarly, a lack of time to repay a loan hurts your record. Now there is no excuse for this, as the automatic debits of the cards pay for you, of course if you activate this option on your platform. If you have a service, for example, a cell phone plan and you don't pay for it or you do it at the wrong time, you throw out your history. That payment that you had to make for the Internet service that they offer you and you forgot to pay, is also a point against you.

There are few cases, but it happens that a duplicate identity is the cause of a bad credit history. Believe it or not, there are eight identities known as my first name and first surname all over the country. And, yes, because of the confusion of those names, your credit history may be affected. A fatal consequence of not paying debts on time is that, although it sounds very cruel, it is more difficult to access some jobs. The truth is that certain companies condition the hiring of workers, in the sense that they do not have a bad rating in the central risk of the country or are reported at a loss.

2.5. How many days of late payment am I allowed and how does this impact my credit history?

2.5.1. Normal. If you haven't been late any day, this would be your credit score; you're a candidate for a loan, according to the banks. If, despite your payments, you don't have this rating, it could be because you were less than six months late. In six months, after you catch up on your accounts, you may qualify as normal.

2.5.2. Client with potential problems. That's how you qualify if you're 9 to 30 days late. You only pay the installment and continue your punctual payments the following months to get back to a normal qualification. With this rating, you still have access to personal loans, although not to large sums of money, and your interest rate will be a little higher.

2.5.3. Deficient customer. You enter this category with more than 30 days and less than 60 days delay. You will not be able to receive new loans from any bank.

2.5.4. Doubtful client. When your late payment is more than 60 days and less than 120. You are not solvent enough to pay interest.

2.5.5. Bankrupt client. Your debt repayment delay is more than 120 days. You've suspended your payments. Get ready, it's the worst credit rating. Banks see it as unlikely that you will recover, so the idea of a loan is unlikely.

Other ways to ruin your credit history are to use your credit card for supposed rebates (which you'll eventually forget) and not to calculate budgets when applying for credit for an important event (such as travel or your wedding).

2.6. Is the credit information deleted at some point?

Historical information keeps popping up. For example, in August 2016 I had the debt I referred to in previous lines; I had a couple of delays in my payments with a minimum amount. That will not be erased, it will always appear, although no longer as a debtor.

2.7. How do I repair my credit history?

Understand and understand your credit report and credit rating. This is a record of your financial past. Include any loans, bills, credit cards or other debts you may have had and whether you made the proper payments to each account. To sum up: if I have a $9500 credit in my bank and I ask for $9000, I am risking too much to be qualified as a potential danger. On the other hand, if I apply for about $5,000, have backing money and pay the installments on time, you will see that I am potentially subject to more loans.

2.7.2. Review your credit report periodically. To detect unauthorized activity, errors and unpaid invoices. Request a free copy of your credit report on your country's credit report page. Establish a deadline and budget for paying your debts and contact all creditors to agree on payment deadlines.

What I will tell you next is something that happened to me with one of my debit cards. I was alarmed, asked for a report at the nearest bank I could find, and actually recorded that I withdrew $300. Then, I made a request for a refund; I wrote down the references of the teller who gave me another figure. They responded to me after a short time. They accepted that the poor calibration of their ATM was what caused the problem. I got my money back.

Another example, which I am very embarrassed to present (now I have it clearer), is that I did not want to review my credit report because I thought (very naively) that if I paid the minimum amount of credit, it would decrease. Serious mistake, which I will explain in the next point.

2.8. Be cautious if creditors propose to "reduce" or "skip" payments. It's better to refinance

Paying a minimal amount, although apparently better than not paying at all, is a small trap. Because, even if you cover the minimum amount so that your account is considered current and does not generate interest, it is also a trap that will cause the balance on your card to convert, grow until it is almost unpayable. Why? Because of the way it's calculated and applied. Suppose your credit card balance is $10000 and your credit limit is $30000. There are two methods that can be applied:

- $10000 (credit limit) x 1.25% (factor) = $375 minimum payment. The first is based on your line of credit. The bank takes 1.25% of your total line of credit and sets the amount to pay.

- $10000 (balance) x 1.5% (factor) = $150 + $320 (VAT + interest) = $470 minimum payment. The second is the sum of 1.5% of the balance owed to the bank plus interest on this amount with VAT.

Your minimum payment is $470, whichever is greater. You would be applying a payment of only $150 to your debt and almost 70% would be used to pay interest. If you keep paying that minimum bill, your debt will grow every month and the minimum payment will go up until your ability to pay won't allow you to cover even that amount. Cancel delinquent accounts first, then debts with the highest interest rates; you can save money. The example of my mismanagement of money and minimum card payments caused a debt in my budget. And I don't want you to repeat that bad example.

As for refinancing your debt, deal with the bank to reschedule your credit payment over the next six months. When you fall behind on your payments, even if it's for a month, your immediate option is to request to refinance your debt. The problem with applying for this is that your credit score will change negatively and stay that way for the next six months.

2.8.1. Consider a debt consolidation credit or balance transfers to a lower-interest credit card. It's about simplifying your monthly payments into a single payment, resulting in a lower monthly payment. It is aimed at people with a credit card debt that generally has higher interest rates. If you have a home or other valuable property that you can use as collateral, you risk losing it if you can't repay the loan. This type of credit could reduce your monthly payment, but increase the total amount you pay over the life of the loan. Paying more than the minimum amount can help you pay off the loan faster. It's kind of hard to find. In some countries "debt buying" between one bank and another is popular; interest rates are variable, but it guarantees that you have everything in one account.

2.8.2. You could save money. You may be able to pay off your debts in less time. For example, a full-time job, more consultancies (in which you develop your specialty and can give in a particular way) and extra payments for bonuses and overtime can make a good mattress for what you're looking to acquire, even if you go little by little. But you can, you can.

There are ways to save. One of the most eye-catching is *kakeibo*, a Japanese savings method that involves the use of a notebook. It records, at the beginning of each month, income and fixed expenses, such as mortgage or rent, electricity, self-assessment, among others. This way, you can know how much money you have left over for the rest of your expenses during the month.

Every time we make a purchase or pay something, we must write down the day and the corresponding section. If the expense has to do with food, leisure, clothes, etc., it must be constant and meticulous. You can't leave anything unrecorded, no matter how small the expense, or it won't do any good. The key is planning and control. At the end of each week and month, you'll be able to add your expenses by category and see if you've reached your monthly savings goal. This way, you will be able to correct your behaviors for the next month. Several examples and comments in forums suggest the success of this method, achieving savings of up to $200 a month without going through needs.

Saving money at the bank means that the bank will not charge you withdrawal fees or for not having a minimum amount in your account at the end of each month. In addition, these entities pay interest on your money, according to the amount you have deposited. Obviously, the more money, the higher the interest. Although you won't be able to make a living from the interest the bank gives you, because it's not that high. Something very different happens if you save in the so-called rural boxes or in the financial ones, which have and offer the best remunerations to the deposits of more than 360 days.

2.8.3. You are looking for a credit counseling agency. To get the best services, rates and plans, as well as ensure their legitimacy. Many credit counselors offer their services through local offices, on the Internet or by phone. Try to find an organization that offers in-person counseling services. Once you develop a list of potential credit counseling organizations, check their reputation by asking this list of questions: What services do you offer, do you offer me information, do you help me solve my immediate problem, do you help me develop a plan to avoid problems in the future, what are your charges or fees, what will happen if I cannot pay the charges or make contributions, will I have a formal written agreement or contract with you, are you licensed to offer services in the state where I live, what are the qualifications of your counselors, are they accredited or certified by an outside organization?

The provincial savings banks in some countries are a source of reliable advice, as their main purpose is to promote savings among families, provide loans to entrepreneurs and promote cultural activities. Both client and advisor agree to reach an acceptable credit between them.

2.8.4. Pay your bills on time. After some time, this will positively affect your credit score and creditworthiness. Never forget to write it in your diary or use an alarm app to remind you of the days missing for payment.

2.8.5. Be careful when closing accounts. Because it can negatively affect your credit score by reducing your credit history or decreasing your available credit; close the account in which you have the lowest available balance. Contact the bank by phone and then in person. Verify that there are no outstanding debts or commitments to the bank. It notes that accounts that have not been properly closed continue to generate debts. It is advisable to wait a while between the opening of a new account and the cancellation of the old one to check that the receipts and payroll are correctly charged to the new account. Be patient enough, cancellation of a card takes a month or more. After this time, request a copy of your credit report to make sure the account is classified as "closed.

If the account appears open, call the bank's customer service to report the error, send a letter by certified mail (including a copy of your original letter requesting the account to be closed), and then verify your credit report again. An example of how it would affect:

A person has two credit card accounts. A has a balance of $500 and a limit of $2000. B has a zero balance, because it is not in use, and a $3000 cap.

Total balances = 500+0=500.

Appropriations authorized = 2000 + 3000 = 5000.

Credit utilization rate = 500/5000 = 10%.

If you close or cancel the card you do not use, the usage rate rises to 25% because you are closing the available or authorized credit. This higher rate hurts your credit score. When you close the B card account:

Total balances = 500 +0=500.

Appropriations authorized = 2000 + 0 = 2000.

Credit usage rate = 500/2000 = 25% (rising).

Closing two available credit cards affects credit score.

2.8.6. Plan ahead for major purchases. Whether it's a home, vehicle or other important item, high credit scores make borrowers enjoy lower interest rates and higher credit limits. Try to improve your credit score within six months. To do this, plan ahead if you want to buy.

Another anecdote. I have a line of credit with a bank for $5000, and so it was three long years. My mother had a very risky and great idea: I lent her $2500 from my line of credit and she deposited it on time for the six months in which she requested the installments to pay that amount. Result: My credit line increased to $9500. Now I can have more credit on my line.

In the case of the acquisition of a property, it is not only this. Consider the fact that you're acquiring a small piece of our national territory. This applies in the case of an apartment or *penthouse*. At present, the metropolises of different countries are becoming filled with people, spaces that before nobody gave a value and now they do due to the arrival of a group of investors. This is a consequence of the demand of people who want to reach their workplaces, which make more apartments in very small spaces. Other real estate investments are largely funded by the State, with the respective consideration of the environment.

A case in some countries regarding the real estate offer are programs for real state developing in rural areas, let's call it "My Housing Fund". A state-sponsored real estate program to purchase a home that incorporates sustainability criteria in its design and construction, thereby reducing the impact on the environment. These funds grant the bonus as a percentage (3% or 4%) that is deducted from the financing value, according to the degree of sustainability, for the acquisition of this type of housing. The potential owner turns to a financial institution for an assessment of his or her ability to pay. It is in the bank where you can apply for it.

Another example is the case of the beginning of the school year in some Latin American countries between the months of March and April. School supplies lists are a nightmare for parents with school-age children. One solution is to buy part of the list wholesale from several parents, or borrow a campaign-focused loan at a lower interest rate than credit cards.

2.8.7. Don't get into debt beyond your means. Try not to borrow amounts you can't repay within 60 days. Of your monthly salary, you should only spend a maximum of between 30% and 40% for the payment of debts.

Some time ago I learned a formula that I found on various websites; it is called the rule of 20, 30 and 50. It is that 50% of your salary is used to cover your most basic expenses, such as transportation tickets or supplies to mobilize your car, food, payment of services and taxes; 20% for savings in case of emergency and 30% for your personal expenses. Always take care of this valuable rule.

2.9. I increased my credit history

As you will be aware, the various bodies responsible for regulating and supervising the financial, insurance and private pension systems of each country are obliged to record all the information on the entities they supervise: banks, cooperatives, finance companies, savings banks. They also have an obligation to report when their customers stop paying credits, cards, or keep accounts in overdraft.

Each time these entities handle a payment default dispute, they submit a report. Commercial companies and educational entities also report to private risk centers. They collect all the information for their customers, that is, anyone who wants to consult. Every time they look at your I.D., they'll see what you are financially.

A curiosity happened to me when I bought a new telephone line. The number was previously in the name of another person, whom we will call John Smith. For about two years, a well-known appliance store called my number looking for this Juan Perez. I can't imagine how much your credit history has diminished.

2.9.1. Pay on time. Bills, credit cards, personal and mortgage loans, utilities, cell phones, taxes, checks, bills of exchange, alimony. Use "automatic debit," a service that allows you to pay your bills automatically using a savings or checking account, as long as there is money in the account.

2.9.2. Control your expenses. So that at the end of the month you have a balance in your bank account. Another short anecdote on how to control expenses. There was a time when I didn't have a steady job. In that period I went to a fair allusive to cats (I have several as pets). He wanted to buy a specialized hairbrush; he had to spend $70 for one. I found the instrument plus other elements, which would not necessarily serve my cats. At the end of the visit to the fair, I had to pay for everything $200. That month I had to control the expenses of my expenses.

2.9.3. Following the previous step, if you don't already have one, open a checking account. This type of account has a couple of additional services: you can make use of the virtual channels and you will have an overdraft quota, which is a kind of credit. If you don't have cash and you have to make a payment, you can withdraw money from your account even if you don't have it. That money earns interest (expensive) and you have up to 30 days to pay it.

In addition, you will be able to make free transfers to savings accounts and make withdrawals and deposits with checks from other entities without incurring other expenses, avoiding the dangers of carrying physical money. Part of the entities' evaluation is the relationship between the available credit quotas and the use you make of them; under overdraft use translates into "good management" and, therefore, the rating will be good.

2.9.4. Increase the quota of your card or ask for a new one. This will have an effect on the quota credit/use of credit ratio. Use your cards wisely, neither 100% nor 0%. We will talk about credit cards in the following sections.

2.9.5. Get an increase in your credit limit, it will improve your credit rating. It is enough to gather the documentation that supports the reasons why you should be given a credit increase (a salary increase, for example). Argument your case. However, keep in mind that a request for an increase in the credit limit may cause your credit score to drop some points.

2.10. Overcoming Credit Card Debt

Before getting into this, read all the credit card terms and conditions carefully. In this way, you will avoid disappointment and be attentive to what is to come.

2.10.1. Avoid withdrawing cash from credit cards. In particular, to pay off credit cards or other debts. This was one of the reasons I got into debt, as I said at the beginning. When I wanted cash, while I wasn't getting my salary, I got $10, $20 or $30; they always charged me $9. That's how I got on the biggest debt of my life.

2.10.2. Sign up for a new credit card. Consider that possibility as you lead your daily life. The call centers of the various banks will look for you and it will be your turn to choose.

If you have too much credit card debt, getting another credit card is not the answer. However, if you need to increase your credit score quickly, this may be your only option. Try to get a card with a 0% intro balance transfer option, which will allow you to transfer your existing debt and rest from paying interest each month. If you can't get approval for credit cards because of your low score, look for a secured credit card.

2.10.4. Keep the cards open. Because each continues to contribute to your credit history. In fact, many people mistakenly believe that closing credit card accounts will help their credit score, when it is likely to have the opposite effect. The longer your accounts have, the more they will add to your score. Even if you no longer use your old credit cards, you can cut the cards or block them but don't cancel them. This happened to me with a credit card from an appliance store, I blocked it from use but didn't cancel it. This increased my credit history.

2.10.5. Compare different types of cards. Prepaid credit cards are not reported to major credit bureaus and will not help increase your credit score. However, a secured credit card can help improve your score. This is a credit card with a guarantee (which becomes the credit limit), which can improve your credit rating; as long as you use it responsibly. It is convenient for me to use a certain card from a certain bank because others raise my interest rate, which does not benefit my credit history.

2.10.6. Mix your forms of credit. An example is the opening of a store credit card and its use for some purchases. These types of cards can improve your credit score, albeit slightly. These will help you resist the urge to spend on other things and accumulate rewards, such as free gas. Pay the balance immediately after each use and your credit score will reflect your good credit history, payment history and increase in available credit. A good use could be an afternoon of possible payable purchases or a dinner that you will cancel immediately to keep your card active. Negotiate with the bank, be assertive for new loans.

Be careful when combining business and private accounts, because personal loans can only help you to a certain extent and your business will exceed the financial resources linked to your assets, which will diminish your financial stability. When you choose business loans you give your company the option of developing a strong financial history, which will allow you to secure larger and more complex loans in the future. These have better conditions with rates that can go from 8 to 12%, against those of a personal whose percentages can be between 45 and 50% annually. There is no way to know ahead of time how a certain action will affect your credit history, because the figure depends on the unique information within the credit report.

2.11. Keep your credit history this way

2.11.1. Limit your accounts. Many store and/or credit cards can lower your credit score, even if you don't use the accounts and pay the balances in full. Block the cards, but don't overdo the shopping.

2.11.2. Use your accounts. Make purchases and pay the entire balance each month. In this way, you keep the balance-limit ratio low. Using less than the available credit limit will help increase your credit score. The little shopping, you know.

2.11.3. Pay your bills on time. Lenders consider your payment records to establish your reliability. Always remember this.

2.11.4. Use credit cards regularly and responsibly. For small purchases and pay the balance at the end of the month. This shows that you can borrow small amounts of money and can be trusted to repay them when you cancel your accounts at the end of the month. So pay on time.

2.11.5. Keep your job, venture, and/or primary residence for two years or more. Lenders use this information to determine your stability. Responsibility is worth even a *freelance* venture. The truth is that nowadays a stable job is not enough and the creation of a company generates income from your knowledge.

2.11.6. Continue to review your credit report. That way you could detect unauthorized activity and errors. Report any inconvenience immediately. Never neglect it. Always schedule a few days to review the report over the Internet.

2.11.7. Get a loan that you can easily repay. If you know you can afford it, a personal loan can improve your credit rating. For example, a loan to pay for mobile equipment in five months.

2.11.8. Use your resources. If you have a home but have gone into debt, check to see if the value of the property has increased recently. You can borrow money from your home equity to get a small loan, which will increase your credit rating. The parents of the friend who lent me the money to pay my debt mortgaged her home to start her business. After 12 years, they were able to get their house back. Ask a family member for help. You may know someone who has better credit than you and can help you in this situation. Ask him to be the guarantor of your loan. This will guarantee the bank that the loan will be repaid and give you the opportunity to show reliability. Give that guarantee by paying on time.

2.11.9. Optimize your credit usage rate. If you have multiple credit cards and debts on each, cards with high limit debt ratios are penalized more in your credit score than cards with lower limit debt ratios. You already know that ideal credit usage rates are below 10% and that you can transfer debt from one card to another to help accommodate credit usage. Consider whether you would have to accept higher interest rates, use all your possibilities.

It is important to add that among the things you should pay for with your credit card are airfare, hotels, cruises or other types of travel, as they offer benefits that can help you save money and protect you from losses. Purchasing a new mobile phone with credit cards provides extended warranties and protection against theft and damage for the first 90 to 120 days after you purchase the item.

Also, the credit card is useful to pay in advance for goods or services that you will receive later. In the event that delivery of the product or service you pay for is cancelled, your card issuer will reimburse you for the purchase. With some credit cards you can receive additional points and miles for cable, electricity and Internet bills. Keep in mind that the credit card is not the extension of your money, because it is an amount that the bank lends you and you must return. Nor is it to pay for purchases in dozens of installments, but between three or six. This way, you won't increase the final amount of your acquisitions.

Chapter 3. Tips for Taking Advantage of Financial Freedom (even more)

If you have several debts, you loose control over them and ignore what interest and many other things you are paying. It is important that you create a payment plan. Only you can identify how much money you receive and how much you can pay more each month. Avoid spending to impress people; make sense of financial spending. Are you sure you need that 60-inch television more than new clothes for your job, books for your knowledge or a training course? The credit card cannot be seen as a temptation.

You can share expenses. I've seen several young people and adults share common spaces. So-called *roommates* share the rent of space, some services, transportation, food and more. Create more sources of income! And if you don't believe them, put that credit card away. There are people who sell their products and services through the Internet. Find out how you can turn your hobby into passion and talent. From being a *community* business *manager*, I now sell my images online, offer pet grooming services near my home, especially cats and more.

Look for mentors to help you discover your financial intelligence, as well as books to educate you on it. Invest your money. How? First you have to know that there is no investment without risk; find out if you are a risky, conservative or moderate investor. You're not going to get money fast. Some investments will generate the first income after a few months and others after a few years. In addition, investments may depend on macroeconomic and other external factors.

I suggest that you invest the extra money you have saved and that you can lose without being affected. Investment funds or long-term deposits are a good way to start. Another good option is the board, which aims to help each other with savings and investment. This group of people contribute (periodically) an amount of money called a quota to form a "bag", which is allocated to one of the previously elected members. It all starts with the person who touches you that month and so on until everyone gets their money. There are no interest rates, but there is mutual trust.

If you don't have an emergency fund, don't use your credit card in case you're presented with one. How will you then cover the debt you've created for yourself? To think about it and digest it. If you want to get out of debt more quickly, you should know your total amount owed. Don't act ignorant or procrastinate the amount of the month until the last day of payment, don't do it. Classify them by total amount owed, which comes from the sum of the interest rate, additional charges, how much is the minimum monthly payment, total debt, and how many months the debt is deferred. Sell unused items that are in good condition, such as visually pleasing coffee pots, books, decorative objects; with the goal of recovering some money. Cancel the services you don't need, such as *streaming* television, clubs to which your presence is limited to once or twice a year; which is actually a hole for your economy.

With the exchange rate in our country, exporters and those who have savings or investments in foreign currency are the first to benefit. When a credit is requested in dollars and you have income in national currency, the exchange of currency necessary to make payments generates a beneficial balance for the bank. This is because the selling price of the dollar is not the same as the buying price. Keep in mind the exchange rate. A dollar loan is convenient when the value of this currency decreases. This is not stable and may alter your finances if the price of that currency rises suddenly. You have to be careful, especially when it comes to personal loans.

Don't speculate on the trend of foreign currency; diversify your savings and investments in currencies. When time deposits and mutual funds are in both soles and dollars, foreign exchange risk is avoided. Also, reduce your debt in dollars. Keep in mind that you will receive your pension in national currency.

Before you lend money to your friend, neighbor, partner or a specific person, keep in mind that lending money by word of mouth is not a valid option; you have to draw up a contract to force the other person, if he refuses to pay you, to comply with the agreement. You can find out through various platforms how the economy of the person you plan to lend money to is. If that person has large debts with the bank, lenders, municipal banks, *online* stores ... I recommend that you do not lend money. Who guarantees that you will return it?

What should not be missing in the loan contract with someone:

- Your name and the name of the person you want to lend money to (their identity documents).
- The amount you're going to lend.
- The time the other person has to give it back to you.
- The way he'll pay you back.
- The schedule in which payments will be made.
- Interests, if any.
- The signature, with the notarial certification.
- A promissory note.

It is never too much to ask for any guarantee to ensure the return of your money.

It is important to keep in mind that there are always fraudulent operations. One of the best known is the Ponzi scheme. This scheme constitutes a fraudulent investment operation based on the payment of interest to investors with their own or other investors' invested money. First, we seek to invent a financial product that involves an investment. They present it to people saying that if they invest money in it, they will be able to charge quite high interest rates, much higher than with any traditional product. Those who do not suspect this fraud will invest expecting large amounts.

When the number of investors is increasing, those who come after seeing that those who have invested before getting the promised money. These people receive the amount, but that profit does not have the origin explained to them; it comes from the amounts contributed by new investors and even by themselves. In this way, the first ones to arrive are the ones who win the most and it only works when new people or candidates to be duped appear. One realizes that scheme by the percentage of interest, since the interests that are promised are much higher than those offered by any other product. In addition, it is not well recognized what is being sold to make profits.

An example of this is something very curious that happened in some countries. Three renowned Peruvian entertainment artists, the popular "participants of telereality contest programs", promoted a "very profitable marketing network" that was actually a scam. According to several newspapers in some countries, in order to be part of that network one must register paying an initial fee of $225 and then a monthly amount of $160. Supposedly, this investment could yield a profit of more than $25,000. Not to believe it. A television program covering the entertainment section invited an economist to clarify the issue. Of course, the scheme proposed by the television figures constituted a scam. The economist said they can be left with a return below what was invested and that the capital is taken by the marketing network.

He also assured that the network is a "pyramidal structure" in which if you don't carry people, you lose all your money and there is no institution you can claim. And who did these guys use of telereality? To their naive fans, who had no idea what their idols were promoting. Although the artists defended themselves, the matter had visibility for a long time. So much so that even the body in charge of the regulation and supervision of financial systems in some countries warned the general public to be careful about participating in this type of business, because they could lose their savings.

Chapter 4. Final Advice

One of the tools you can use to your advantage is the free investment or personal loan; however, it has certain restrictions. Never buy a car with this type of credit, since there is a specific credit for it. A car loan has more convenient interest rates and benefits than a personal loan. It is also not good for paying off another credit, except for the famous "debt purchase". Don't enter the so-called "carousel", in other words, do not take out one loan to pay off another, unless it is a debt consolidation: take out a loan to pay off several debts and keep just one. It is also not recommended to complete the down payment on a home loan; always save for that type of purchase.

You shouldn't lend to other people; even though you know them, they're not you and they can probably fail to pay on time. Easier to repay that loan? Get lower rates by opening an account in the chosen entity, especially if it is an account where your credits are saved; you would have access to lower interest rates. It helps to have a credit card from that entity. A good way to reduce interest on your loan is to pay extraordinary fees, that is, pay double fees in some month and generate savings. Remember: having pre-approved loans and cards is a good indicator in your credit history; for different entities you are a low risk person and you have a solvent economic situation.

If you are denied of getting a credit, is maybe because it exceeds your possibility to pay or maybe you cannot prove that you have enough incomes to pay for it. Ask for the reason of the denial. In this way, you will be able to see the improvements you can make, such as reducing your debts and pending loans to settle, increasing your income for a greater possibility to pay, or revisiting your credit report to request again the amount to be borrowed.

There are other important things to consider, like investing in your professional and personal growth, project goals, use the 50-20-30 system that we explained in previous lines, have a general balance of income and expenses, get out of the comfort zone, stop envying and complaining. All of these habits will allow you to improve financially, while your credit history benefits.

You must save money. If you want to see your money grow, you have to make sacrifices. Find all the ways to make a living. Let me give you an example. I have a *coach*, who warned me that two health conditions are the most expensive: coronary heart disease and mental health-related illnesses. Even if you have a humble job, you will have to save for one or both conditions. I won't tell you which one I have, but I can assure you that the cost of medicines and private medical consultation is high.

Quit the job you have. Currently, a stable job in some countries is not secure. There are many graduated people in my profession and every day there are more staff cuts in the workplaces. Entrepreneurship is the key. As an example from my parents, my mother is an obstetrician and my dad is an electronic technician and chauffeur. One day they stopped being employees of the government and started several entrepreneurships: private transportation, a convenience store, food concessionaire, lender, home installations. These ventures have brought them more income than their careers. Today, they continue to invest in real estate while receiving residual income from rentals of apartments and shops.

One of my grandparents worked in a textile factory for 40 years as a machine technician. Even though he bought two houses he worked for 40 years. He worked even on holidays, didn't saw his family as much as he wanted to and had to rest after so many years of work. I particularly, bid farewell to an expensive lifestyle: I bid farewell to that pitcher with the head of a cat and to that luxurious first-class journeys. Finally: Bill Gates, Mark Zuckerberg, Steve Jobs, Michael Dell, left their comfortable life and set out on their own path. And you, what do you need to start creating your financial freedom? It's up to you.

CPSIA information can be obtained
at www.ICGtesting.com
Printed in the USA
BVHW040954030220
571272BV00025B/1964